TRAINING FOR
HARVEST

TRAINING FOR
HARVEST

Stopping for the One,
BELIEVING FOR THE MULTITUDES

ROLLAND & HEIDI BAKER

DESTINY IMAGE® PUBLISHERS, INC.

P.O. Box 310, Shippensburg, PA 17257-0310

"Promoting Inspired Lives."

This book and all other Destiny Image and Destiny Image Fiction books are available at Christian bookstores and distributors worldwide.

Cover design by Eileen Rockwell

Interior design by Terry Clifton

For more information on foreign distributors, call 717-532-3040.

Reach us on the Internet: www.destinyimage.com.

ISBN 13 TP: 978-0-7684-1078-5

ISBN 13 eBook: 978-0-7684-1079-2

For Worldwide Distribution, Printed in the U.S.A.

1 2 3 4 5 6 7 8 / 21 20 19 18 17

"Blessed are the poor in spirit,
for theirs is the kingdom of heaven."
—Matthew 5:3

CONTENTS

INTRODUCTION

"Love. It is a small four-letter word that will cost you everything—laying down your life, passion and compassion, giving without expecting, feeling His very heartbeat and surrendering to His rhythm, and following the Lamb wherever He goes."
—Heidi Baker

As Christian missionaries we are to be committed to expressing a living and tangible response to those commandments that Jesus called greatest: *"Love the Lord your God with all your heart and with all your soul and with all your mind and with all your strength,"* and *"Love your neighbor as yourself"* (Mark 12:30-31). The Spirit of God has asked us to make this love concrete in the world, incarnate in our thoughts, our bodies, our lives, and our every action. We are to exist to participate in bringing the kingdom of God to earth in all its aspects, but most especially through our particular calling to serve the very poor—the destitute, the lost, the broken, and the forgotten.

> *The King will reply, "I tell you the truth, whatever you did for one of the least of these brothers of Mine, you did for Me"* (Matthew 25:40).

Missions is built around the application of the Gospel to some of the most desperate economic and spiritual circumstances on earth, with all the boldness of which we, in Christ, are capable.

Many of you will be been sent to places where "love" must mean bread for the hungry, water for the thirsty, and healing for the sick every day. It must mean family for the orphan, freedom for the captives, and peace for the war-torn. You must desire always to make your love real in these ways for as long as the poor are with us.

As you seek to display God's heart in the outpouring of this love, you will find that you are also constantly blessed by a great many treasures uncovered in the hearts of those you are sent to serve. An important part of your calling is to share these treasures with the whole body of Christ with the great hope that every one of your trials, your testimonies, and your victories may in turn become life and encouragement for the entire Church, *"until we all reach unity in the faith and in the knowledge of the Son of God"* (Eph. 4:3).

Part One

WHO GOD IS

JESUS IS OUR GOAL

Rolland Baker

*"But seek first His kingdom and His righteousness, and
all these things will be given to you as well."*
—MATTHEW 6:33

SESSION SUMMARY

For Heidi and myself, our daily goal in life is to find Jesus and seek after Him and then keep finding more of Him. We think the most exciting aspect of the Christian life is that every day we get to wake up in the morning able to find more of Jesus. He personally is more interesting to us than anything on this earth. Honestly, we should all be fighting to spend time with Jesus. Once you give up on seeking Him, what's left? Nothing! Jesus is the prize, the bread that came down from heaven, the way and the truth and the life. He is the greatest thing about salvation and heaven. He is the author of life and He makes Himself available to us.

Jesus is often the most unpopular and controversial person in the Church. We want miracles, we want theology, we want results, we want recognition; we want lots of things, but we don't seem to be that interested in Jesus. And yet, without Him none of these things are possible. When we fix our eyes on Jesus, the author and perfecter of our faith, and determine, like Paul, to know nothing but Christ crucified, then we come to understand that missions is first and foremost about Jesus. It is out of our intimacy with Him that we are able to be intimate with others.

What God has done through Iris did not begin with a human program or a carefully constructed plan. It came about because we abandoned ourselves in love to seek the face of Jesus, desiring intimacy, communication, and companionship with Him and sharing in His love for righteousness. **We begin and end each day with total dependence on God in the face of great need, and a willingness to go anywhere where the poor and needy are.** In the midst of His supernatural signs and wonders we accept that we will suffer hardship, all the while knowing that the joy of the Lord is our strength. Exulting in the truth and reality of our salvation renders us more capable of compassion for others because we are unfettered by our own sorrows. Outside of surrender to the Holy Spirit in all things, and complete abandonment to the river of God in all decisions and needs, we have no firm design or plan for missions. Jesus is our all in all. *"He* *who did not spare His own Son, but gave Him up for us all—how will He not also, along with Him, graciously give us all things?"* (Romans 8:32).

MAIN CONCEPTS FROM SESSION ONE

*"But seek first His kingdom and His righteousness, and
all these things will be given to you as well."*
—Matthew 6:33

JESUS IS OUR GOAL

Rolland Baker

Seeking and Finding Jesus: *"Now devote your heart and soul to seeking the Lord your God."*
—1 Chronicles 22:19

- *"The kingdom of God is not a matter of talk but of power"* (1 Cor. 4:20). Heal the sick, raise the dead, cleanse the lepers, cast out demons.

- Miracles bring the lost to Jesus, not apologetics.

The Love of God: *"I was found by those who did not seek Me: I revealed Myself to those who did not ask for Me."* —Romans 10:20

- God comes to whomever He chooses, even those who are not seeking Him.

- Never treat salvation lightly—the wages of sin lead to eternal death and hell.

- True repentance must be sought and taught.

Core Values: *"If you belonged to the world, it would love you as its own. As it is, you do not belong to the world, but I have chosen you out of the world."* —John 15:19

- Every ministry needs core values.

- Core values should always be based on the foundation of Scripture and the person of Jesus Christ.

- The Spirit of God will impose His core values in His time and His way.

What Core Values Are Not: *"We who worship by the Spirit of God, who glory in Christ Jesus, and who put no confidence in the flesh."* —Philippians 3:3

- Questions to ask when determining what your core values are *not*:
  - Is Jesus your prize?

- Is He the reason you live?
- Is He the point of everything?

Jesus is what we get out of missions—not changing the world. Not building churches. Not improving the economy. Not planting farms. Not "making a difference."

You Should Not Be a Christian Missionary If... *"Do not conform any longer to the pattern of this world, but be transformed by the renewing of your mind. Then you will be able to test and approve what God's will is—His good, pleasing and perfect will."* —Romans 12:2

- Don't be a Christian missionary if you are not willing to die the very first day for Jesus; if you could do anything else; if you could serve someone other than Jesus; if you are more in love with someone or something other than Jesus.

Is Jesus Enough? *"Now the Lord is the Spirit, and where the Spirit of the Lord is, there is freedom."* —2 Corinthians 3:17

- Under God's control we can experience the greatest freedom.

- Being interested in God and being "fed" by Him should be what satisfies us.

- God's presence must be enough to sustain us in the mission field, even in the face of great evil.

Session One Devotions

SEEKING AND FINDING JESUS

"Now devote your heart and soul to seeking the Lord your God."
—1 CHRONICLES 22:19

Many people want to know what the main emphasis of the Bible is. I believe the main emphasis of the Bible is Jesus Himself, and He is reflected in His command to heal the sick, raise the dead, cleanse the lepers, and cast out demons. As the king He is still the point of His kingdom. We are sent out to exercise the power of God because *"the kingdom of God is not a matter of talk but of power"* (1 Cor. 4:20). The Scriptures reveal that evangelism in the New Testament took place as the result of miracles. It occurred not just because of talk and friendship, but because the love and power of God were demonstrated through the miraculous.

All that being said, will just getting out there and doing what Jesus did sustain you on the mission field in the midst of the poorest of the poor? What if not everyone is healed? What about your own heart? The answers to these questions and many others begin with Jesus. Jesus is the main idea, the main value that keeps us going. He is the One we would die for.

The only place life exists is in Jesus.

> *That which was from the beginning, which we have heard, which we have seen with our eyes, which we have looked at and our hands have touched—this we proclaim concerning the Word of life. The life appeared; we have seen it and testify to it, and we proclaim to you the eternal life, which was with the Father and has appeared to us. We proclaim to you what we have seen and heard, so that you also may have fellowship with us. And our fellowship is with the Father and with His son, Jesus Christ. We write this to make our joy complete* (1 John 1:1–4).

The Word became flesh. Life itself appeared. Can anything else take precedence over this truth? Our goal is always to find Jesus and seek after Him and keep finding more of Him.

REFLECTION QUESTIONS

1. What do you think is the main emphasis of the Bible?

_____

_____

_____

_____

_____
_____
_____
_____
_____
_____
_____
_____

2. Do you believe that Jesus needs to be your goal above all else?

_____
_____
_____
_____
_____
_____
_____
_____
_____
_____
_____
_____
_____

3. How do you "devote your heart and soul" to seeking God?

_____
_____
_____
_____
_____
_____
_____
_____
_____

THE LOVE OF GOD

*"I was found by those who did not seek Me: I revealed
Myself to those who did not ask for Me."*
—Romans 10:20

In Romans 10:20, the apostle Paul is quoting the prophet Isaiah who said this about God: *"I permitted
Myself to be sought by those who did not ask for Me: I permitted Myself to be found by those who did not seek Me.
I said, 'Here am I, here am I,' to a nation which did not call on My name"* (Isa. 65:1 NASB).

In His great love, God came to Jew and Gentile alike, and He continues to come to all equally to
make Himself known even when we are not seeking Him. What great love! What great patience! God
will provoke sinners at all costs because our sinfulness is always overcome by His love. We are born sinners and made clean by the blood of the Lamb. If you want to know Jesus you must first understand who
you are.

Often the biggest issue people have with God is that they don't believe they are sinners who deserve
the punishment of hell. They can't understand how God could possibly be so judgmental when they are
trying to be good, trying to lead a decent life. "How could the judgment of hell be God's position?" they
ask. Under the Old Covenant, those who did not seek the Lord were put to death: *"All who would not seek
the Lord, the God of Israel, were to be put to death, whether small or great, man or woman"* (2 Chron. 15:13).
But thanks be to God we are living in the New Covenant. We have Jesus who bore our sins for us so that
we do not have to take the burden of God's judgment. We need to rejoice in what we have in Jesus while
understanding that while we were still sinners Christ died for us. **The New Covenant doesn't change the
fact that we are born sinners; it just gives us a choice as to the outcome of our sin.**

The message of the Old Testament is not meant to reduce our joy. It is there to teach us God's eternal
truths. Like Israel, who time after time turned away from God only to eventually return, we too find the
open arms of God when we repent. But repentance doesn't just mean saying you're sorry. True repentance
involves a change of heart that can only come from laid-down lovers who cannot be stopped from devot-
ing their heart and soul to seeking the Lord even when it means facing their own sinfulness. We must
never treat salvation lightly.

REFLECTION QUESTIONS

1. What was it like when you first confronted your own sinfulness?

_____
_____
_____
_____
_____
_____
_____
_____

2. What does it mean to have God provoke you, and how does He do that in your life?

_____
_____
_____
_____
_____
_____
_____
_____
_____
_____
_____
_____
_____

3. Where do you find joy in your relationship with Jesus?

_____
_____
_____
_____
_____
_____
_____
_____
_____
_____
_____

CORE VALUES

"If you belonged to the world, it would love you as its own. As it is, you do not belong to the world, but I have chosen you out of the world."
—John 15:19

Every ministry can benefit from a set of core values. These values will differ depending on the ministry, but they should never stray from the foundation of Scripture and the person of Jesus Christ. At Iris we literally live daily by our core values. The genesis of our core values was very much an organic move of God among us. In 2010, we gathered people from Iris bases around the world and sat down together to brainstorm our core values. After much thought and discussion, we narrowed our focus to a set of questions and our answers to those questions. What we came up with turned out to be quite controversial. We found that we were not able to be very ecumenical, or super sensitive, going for the lowest common denominator or the greatest common denominator in an effort to "just get along" with all the other missionary groups here in Mozambique. Our core values have a tendency to ruffle feathers. We have been called weird, a cult, even heretics.

The questions we asked ourselves in pursuit of our core values were hard questions: What keeps us going? What characterizes us? What are we looking for most of all? What motivates us? What are the absolute truths that we would die for? What have we learned from God? Our answers always brought us back to Jesus and Jesus' emphasis in the Bible. The Spirit of God has imposed these values on Iris and it is our job daily to recognize them and adopt them by sheer necessity rather than choice. We share them with you as an example of what we live by with the hope that you may be inspired toward the development of your own core values.

IRIS GLOBAL CORE VALUES

1. **Find God:** We understand that we can find God and can experience intimacy, communication, and companionship with Him in His presence if we share His love for righteousness.

2. **Depend on miracles**: We are totally dependent on Him for everything, and we need and expect miracles of all kinds to sustain us and confirm the Gospel in our ministry.

3. **Go to the least**: We look for revival among the broken, humble, and lowly and start at the bottom with ministry to the poor. God chooses the weak and despised things of the world to shame the proud, demonstrating His own strength and wisdom. Our direction is lower still.

4. **Suffer for Him if necessary**: We understand the value of suffering in the Christian life. Learning to love requires willingness to suffer for the sake of righteousness. Discipline and testing make saints out of us and produce in us the holiness without which we will not see God's face and share His glory. With Paul we rejoice in our weaknesses, for when we are weak we are strong.

5. Rejoice in the Lord: The joy of the Lord is not optional and far outweighs our suffering! In Jesus it becomes our motivation, reward, and spiritual weapon. In His presence is fullness of joy, and with Paul we testify that in all our troubles our joy knows no bounds (see 2 Cor. 7:4). It is our strength and energy without which we die.

REFLECTION QUESTIONS

Before you take time to reflect on the core values of Iris, answer the following questions and then reflect on your answers in light of Iris's core values.

1. What keeps you going?

2. What characterizes you?

3. What are you looking for most of all?

4. What motivates you?

5. What are the absolute truths that you would die for?

6. What have you learned from God?

WHAT CORE VALUES ARE NOT

"We who worship by the Spirit of God, who glory in Christ Jesus, and who put no confidence in the flesh."
—Philippians 3:3

If you are to understand what your personal and corporate ministry values are, it is important to also understand what they are *not* or you might just find yourself on a path that is good enough in the eyes of the world but not what God intends. Scores upon scores of well-meaning people have gone into the mission field with a burning desire to "do good" but have forgotten that it all begins and ends with seeking and finding the One who is goodness itself.

Are you out to change the world, raise the dead, build churches, improve the economy of a poor country, take in orphaned children, plant farms, "make a difference"? Or is Jesus the prize? Is He the reason you live? Is He the point of everything? We don't make use of Jesus to be better missionaries. We don't make use of Him to "do the stuff." We don't make use of Him to experience exciting miracles, signs, and wonders. *He* is the point. **Jesus is what we get out of all of this.**

If Iris did not understand the one essential truth that it all begins and ends with Jesus, we would have given up a long time ago. We would have long ago exhausted ourselves building schools all over Mozambique and planting churches and doing all the work necessary to improve the country. Our hard work alone does not keep us going in the midst of all of the pressures and spiritual warfare. It is Jesus and Him alone that keeps us going. As long as we keep our focus on Him we are able to go forward through today and into tomorrow.

REFLECTION QUESTIONS

1. What currently keeps you going in the Christian life?

_____
_____
_____
_____
_____
_____
_____
_____
_____

_____

2. Identify what your core values are *not*.

_____

3. What path are you currently on right now, and where do you expect it to lead you?

_____

YOU SHOULD NOT BE A CHRISTIAN MISSIONARY IF...

"Do not conform any longer to the pattern of this world, but be transformed by the renewing of your mind. Then you will be able to test and approve what God's will is—His good, pleasing and perfect will."
—Romans 12:2

The only really exciting thing about the Christian life is that every day you wake up in the morning and you get to find more of Jesus. Every day there is the potential to experience something you have never experienced before, and that is true for today, tomorrow, this coming week, and always. We can always learn something about God we never knew before. Every week becomes fresh and spontaneous, more life-giving and less boring. Yet we all know that a lot of people don't think that way. Many tend to think in cliché phrases such as, "He who endures to the end will be saved," and "Hang in there," with the notion that, perhaps, if they hold on with their fingertips to the edge of the cliff and just tough it out, the toughest will win.

The "hard sayings" of Jesus are hard if they are taken as demanding prescriptions for how to live the Christian life. But actually they are descriptions of the Spirit-filled life in which Jesus becomes our righteousness and lives in us, making the impossible demands of Jesus possible and light.

I don't think you should be a Christian if you're not willing to die the very first day for Jesus. I don't think you should be a Christian if you can be anything else. I don't think you should be a missionary if you can possibly do anything else. I don't think you should give to any mission, especially Iris, if you can possibly stand not to. You should certainly not join a mission organization if you can possibly do anything else. As a matter of fact, don't even serve Jesus if you can possibly serve anyone else!

Real love is being so interested in someone that there is no competition. For me, there is no one else I would follow but Jesus. There is nothing else I would do except what I am doing. I'm doing the very thing I want most to do and it's not always easy.

REFLECTION QUESTIONS

1. What is your response to Rolland's statement that you should be willing to die the very first day for Jesus?

----

2. If you could possibly do anything else right now, what would it be?

3. After honestly searching your heart, can you unequivocally state that there is no one else you would rather serve than Jesus? If not, who or what do you want to serve?

4. What is it about Jesus that motivates you towards missions?

IS JESUS ENOUGH?

"Now the Lord is the Spirit, and where the Spirit of the Lord is, there is freedom."
—2 Corinthians 3:17

Today you need to ask yourself the hard question, "What is it that I'm actually interested in?" Do you get upset when it seems like God isn't honoring you or because you don't get something else besides God Himself? We should be all about knowing Him better, not just trying to figure out how to feel better, because being interested in God and getting fed by Him is actually what makes us feel better. God is what satisfies us.

Many of you are excited at the idea of getting rid of everything, jumping on a plane with a one-way ticket and charging off to the most remote and demonized place in the world with never a backward glance. But you need to ask yourself what motivates you. Is your motivation enough to keep you there for thirty years? What happens when you hit bumps in the road, when people not only don't honor you, they actually hate you and would like to kill you? How would you "feel better" in the midst of the most hostile and brutal situations? What is it that would sustain you?

During the reign of David there was a famine in the land for three successive years. David, being a man after God's own heart, responded by seeking the face of the Lord. David was a man of action and he could have chosen to do any number of things in the face of famine, but his *first* response was to seek God. He understood that when God is in control, all things are possible.

The only way to be truly happy is to trust that God is in control and has you on His strings. The greatest relief, the greatest freedom comes when you are under God's control. Think of it—He is in control and you are totally free! Jesus really is enough!

REFLECTION QUESTIONS

1. What is it that you are actually interested in, and where do you see God in this?

---

2. What is your response when you feel God isn't honoring you or when you don't get something besides Him?

3. How do you feel about surrendering complete control to God?

Session Two

THE CENTRALITY OF THE CROSS

Rolland Baker

*"For the joy set before Him He endured the cross, scorning its shame,
and sat down at the right hand of the throne of God."*
—HEBREWS 12:2

SESSION SUMMARY

God's perfection is displayed in the magnificent work accomplished on the cross by Jesus Christ, and He desires that we reap the *full* benefits available to us in the atonement. Jesus didn't die for us to be partial beneficiaries. God wants us to experience the total release and absolute freedom He has for us in Jesus, and in order to do that we must understand that the cross is both seriousness and joy. While the work of the cross is the most profound and significant act known to mankind, **God's perfection on the cross in Jesus is also to be our joy.** Many find this to be a hard teaching, but if you look you will find it in the Scriptures: *"For the kingdom of God is not a matter of eating and drinking, but of righteousness, peace and joy in the Holy Spirit"* (Rom. 14:17). **God wants us to reach out and take hold of the joy that is ours through the Spirit and the Son because we are most pleasing to God when we are pleased *with* Him.** Jesus is delighted to see us rejoice in the reality of our salvation. Some characterize this as foolish levity, but it is in fact a deep work of the Spirit. And it is out of this deep work of the Spirit within our hearts that comes the repentance necessary for the Christian life. In order to appropriate the fullness of our redemption we must possess an awareness of our own need and of Christ's total sufficiency. When we fall deeply in love with Jesus, heaven comes to earth.

What a great salvation we have in Jesus! This is what we must share in the mission field. We carry heaven inside of us and we are made to give it away. Our job among the broken and poor isn't just to meet their physical needs. We are to bring them close to Jesus and then watch to see what He does in response. True revival is born out of an extreme desire for the person of Jesus Christ.

> *Those who had been scattered preached the word wherever they went…and proclaimed the Christ there. When the crowds heard Philip and saw the miraculous signs he did, they all paid close attention to what he said. With shrieks, evil spirits came out of many, and many paralytics and cripples were healed. So there was great joy in that city* (Acts 8:4–8).

MAIN CONCEPTS FROM SESSION TWO

"For the joy set before Him He endured the cross, scorning its shame,
and sat down at the right hand of the throne of God."
—Hebrews 12:2

THE CENTRALITY OF THE CROSS

Rolland Baker

The Cross: God's Perfection: *"For the kingdom of God is not a matter of eating and drinking, but of righteousness, peace and joy in the Holy Spirit, because anyone who serves Christ in this way is pleasing to God and approved by men."* —Romans 14:17-18

- The cross is God's perfection and our source of joy.

- We need both the seriousness of the cross and the joy of the cross.

- It takes childlike faith to exult in the reality of our salvation.

- This deep work of the Spirit brings conviction, repentance, love, gratitude, awe, and wonder.

- The joy found in God's perfection on the cross enables us to withstand the extreme challenges of the mission field.

The Atonement: *"For He bore the sin of many, and made intercession for the transgressors."* —Isaiah 53:12

- What a great salvation we have in Jesus.

- We must learn to appreciate all aspects of the atonement, presenting the full Gospel to everyone.

- A clean conscience is one of God's greatest gifts to us on the cross.

The Purpose and Fruits of Redemption: *"Who has saved us and called us with a holy calling, not according to our works, but according to His own purpose and grace which was granted us in Christ Jesus from all eternity"* —2 Timothy 1:9 NASB

- The grand goal of authentic discipleship is to be conformed to Christ's image.

- "The blood deals with what we have done; redemption deals with what we are" (Watchman Nee).

- We don't go to the poor and the lost and broken just to meet their physical needs.
  - We go to bring the forgotten and wretched close to Jesus, and then we watch to see what He does as He draws close to them in response.

Heaven: *The Goal of Our Faith, the Salvation of Our Souls: "If then you have been raised with Christ, seek the things that are above, where Christ is, seated at the right hand of God. Set your minds on things that are above, not on things that are on earth."* —Colossians 3:2 ESV

- When we rejoice in the midst of suffering, we prove our faith to be genuine, and we obtain the goal of our faith, which is the salvation of our soul.
- Heaven comes to earth not by what we do, but by what Jesus does in us.
- True revival is born out of an extreme desire for the person of Jesus Christ.

Practical Missions: *"I tell you the truth, whatever you did not do for one of the least of these, you did not do for Me."* —Matthew 25:45

- Relationship with the living God is the wellspring of missions.
- The unstoppable fire in our souls is the catalyst for lasting transformation.
- Our ministry in the mission field is to present everyone perfect in Christ, which takes years of hard work, love, and patience.

Sound Doctrine: *"Remember your leaders, who spoke the word of God to you. Consider the outcome of their way of life and imitate their faith."* —Hebrews 13:7

- We need sound doctrine that:
  - Nourishes us (1 Timothy 4:6).
  - Keeps our hearts set on God (1 Timothy 6:3–21).
  - Enables us to preach the full Gospel (2 Timothy 4:3).

Session Two Devotions

THE CROSS: GOD'S PERFECTION

"For the kingdom of God is not a matter of eating and drinking, but of righteousness, peace and joy in the Holy Spirit, because anyone who serves Christ in this way is pleasing to God and approved by men."
—Romans 14:17-18

We in the Church tend to take the cross so lightly. It is seldom preached about, and yet the cross is God's perfection. And if it is God's perfection, then it is our source of joy. "What?" you say? "Joy?" Yes, joy! If we are just heavy and serious all the time, we don't reap the benefits, the total release, the absolute freedom won on the cross. We need both the seriousness of the cross *and* the joy to understand the fullness of the atonement.

Daily we pass through our own brokenness and God's conviction, and thankfully we are not left there. When we embrace the things of God's kingdom—His righteousness, peace, and joy in the Holy Spirit (in that order)—we reap the reward of doing what is right and resisting what is wrong. We become childlike, not childish, totally trusting in our Father in heaven. This is the joy of thinking on what is true. It isn't foolish levity or some kind of cheap silliness. It is exultation in the reality of our salvation, which is a powerful work of the Spirit. It is that deep conviction and repentance that wells up from within in sobs of love and gratitude, mingling with a sense of awe and wonder at His magnificent presence as He baptizes us with His Spirit until joy overtakes us. **It is our joy found in God's perfection displayed on the cross that enables us to withstand the extreme challenges and pressures of the mission field.** Every day we are still learning to love, still learning to go lower still, to stop for the one, to be a friend of God. It all begins and ends with understanding His perfection in the cross.

REFLECTION QUESTIONS

1. How do you currently understand the dichotomy of the cross in your own life?

_____

_____

_____

_____

_____

_____
_____
_____
_____
_____
_____

2. What does it mean to daily need to pass through our own brokenness and God's conviction and then on to that place of life in Christ?

_____
_____
_____
_____
_____
_____
_____
_____
_____
_____
_____
_____

3. How would you describe your current friendship with God?

_____
_____
_____
_____
_____
_____
_____
_____
_____
_____

THE ATONEMENT

"For He bore the sin of many, and made intercession for the transgressors."
—Isaiah 53:12

Stop for a moment and ask yourself why you love God. Most of you will have lots of reasons that have to do with the things God does for you, but what would make you love God so much that you would, without hesitation, give up your life and give up everything you have in this world for Him? The Scriptures say we should consider it all rubbish for the surpassing worth of knowing Jesus Christ, our Lord. What would make you love Him that much?

To answer that question, let's begin with another one: "What it is that makes you unhappy? What causes you the most heart anguish?" A lot of people say it's a guilty conscience that troubles their heart the most because no matter how much you forgive yourself and others forgive you, no one and nothing can erase the fact that you did something wrong. Outside of the atoning work of Jesus on the cross, we are stuck with our guilt and our sin. One of God's greatest gifts to us on the cross is a clean conscience. But how does the atonement give us a clean conscience? Jesus *became* our sin. He took the full wrath of our sins and wiped the slate clean with Himself. Atonement is no trifling matter. God didn't just wave His arm and say, "Oh, you're all forgiven. You can do the most heinous things and we'll just pretend they didn't happen. Everybody gets into heaven." What kind of a world would that be? No, we must understand what sin is, under the full power of the Holy Spirit, in order to appreciate the atonement. The reality of our sin and the magnitude of Jesus' work on the cross cannot be fully understood outside of revelation from God's Spirit.

The only God I'm interested in is the one who can actually cleanse our conscience and take away our sin. That's why I follow Him. That's why He's unique, not just because He's extra nice and extra powerful. There isn't anything greater than redemption—this incredible God who alone has the ability to rescue us from the predicament of our sin. That's how we should present the Gospel as missionaries. Yes, we heal people and we dig wells to give them an introduction to God's love, but above all else we must show them how great a salvation we have in Jesus—how unique Jesus is.

REFLECTION QUESTIONS

1. How would you answer the question, "Why do you love God?"

_____

_____

_____

_____

_____

_____

2. Right now, what is causing you the most heart anguish, and how do you see it in light of the cross?

_____

_____

_____

_____

_____

_____

_____

_____

_____

_____

_____

_____

_____

3. What is your current understanding of _your_ sin in light of the atonement?

_____

_____

_____

_____

_____

_____

_____

_____

_____

_____

_____

_____

THE PURPOSE AND FRUITS OF REDEMPTION

"Who has saved us and called us with a holy calling, not according
to our works, but according to His own purpose and grace which
was granted us in Christ Jesus from all eternity."
—2 Timothy 1:9 NASB

I love that Jesus not only spoke to His disciples about His death on the cross, but He also spoke to them of His *purpose* in dying. Jesus gave His life as a ransom for all, and by that ransom He worked for us our redemption. How great a price He paid! When we talk about the fruit of redemption, remember that we have been redeemed from our lives of evil and have become new creatures in Christ and partakers of the divine nature. A curtain has been drawn on our past, and we now press on to what lies ahead.

We know that Jesus accepted suffering as well as glory. He accepted pain as well as power. The grand goal of authentic discipleship is to be conformed to His image, able to display the same love that He showed. We suffer for the Gospel according to the power of God when we are able, like Jesus, to resist evil opposition with His love. We don't go to the poor and the lost and broken just to meet their physical needs. **We go to bring the forgotten and wretched close to Jesus, and then we watch to see what He does as He draws close to them in response.** It is at that moment that everything changes and all things become possible.

REFLECTION QUESTIONS

1. How do you describe authentic discipleship?

_____

_____

_____

_____

_____

_____

_____

_____

_____

_____

_____

_____

_____

_____

_____

_____

_____

_____

_____

_____

_____

_____

_____

2. Identify a fruit of redemption at work in your own life.

_____

_____

_____

_____

_____

_____

_____

_____

_____

_____

_____

_____

_____

_____

_____

_____

_____

HEAVEN: THE GOAL OF OUR FAITH, THE SALVATION OF OUR SOULS

"If then you have been raised with Christ, seek the things that are above, where Christ is, seated at the right hand of God. Set your minds on things that are above, not on things that are on earth."
—Colossians 3:2 ESV

In heaven there is no spiritual warfare, no poverty, no sickness, no need for disaster relief. On earth we have evil opposition, but in heaven there is no evil opposition. Therefore, perhaps God has different things for us to do down here than He does in heaven. The question is, "What is His will?" What is His purpose on earth for us? So often when people try and answer these questions there is a lack of common sense. Many think God wants us to experience heaven right away, right here and right now. I question that. Yes, Jesus taught us to pray, "On earth as it is in heaven," but Stephen was stoned. Paul was shipwrecked. First Peter spends a whole chapter explaining why we go through trials. The Bible doesn't think it strange that fiery trials come upon us. **Believers all over the world are suffering and yet rejoicing because faith that is genuine and real is more precious than gold.** As we rejoice in the midst of suffering, we are obtaining the outcome of our faith, the goal of our faith, which is the salvation of our souls.

There is a lot of emphasis in the Church on restoring the earth, fixing the earth, changing the world. But is that all the Bible says we are to be doing? The apostle Paul says to set our minds on things above, not on things on earth, because the things that are seen are only temporary. What is unseen is eternal. If we just throw up our hands and say that a good God would never let bad things happen to us, we do not understand God's heart and purposes.

At Iris we would love to see Pemba look like heaven on earth, to see this nation transformed by a mighty visitation from heaven, to see poverty and sickness and evil eradicated. But Jesus said that the kingdom of God is not a physical place. He tells us that the kingdom of God is inside of us. We can all carry heaven inside of us. Outward, physical transformation in Mozambique would be wonderful but it is not enough for our human hearts. Our hearts are hungry for *someone*. We long to experience love, joy, and peace, that perfect love that is beyond expression. We long for God! Many people long for revival yet fail to understand that true revival is born out of an extreme desire for the person of Jesus Christ. **I believe that when we fall deeply in love with Jesus and He sits on the throne of our hearts, heaven begins.**

REFLECTION QUESTIONS

1. What do you think is God's purpose on the earth?

2. How do you view the idea of joy in the midst of suffering?

3. What does revival mean to you?

PRACTICAL MISSIONS

*"I tell you the truth, whatever you did not do for one of
the least of these, you did not do for Me."*
—Matthew 25:45

Heidi and I received a lot of criticism in the early days in Mozambique for being social workers. But we are evangelists as well. We're not just social worker, even though we know that evangelistic meetings don't go very far by themselves when you're preaching to sick, starving people. The apostle Paul said that his goal in all of his work was to present everyone perfect in Christ. We can take a child and feed and clothe them and send them to school, but that is not where it ends. The thrust of ministry is to present everyone perfect in Christ, and we know it takes years of hard work, love, and patience to bring that kind of lasting transformation.

Jesus trained His disciples for three years, yet in the end they didn't know nearly all there was to know. When Jesus was arrested, they didn't understand what was happening. They ran, scared. It wasn't until the Holy Spirit fell on them that the disciples had the courage they needed. And it wasn't until Jesus rose in the air in front of their eyes that the Holy Spirit opened their minds and hearts to understand all that He had said and done. Paul told Timothy to think about these things and that God would give him understanding in everything. We need to press in for the long haul if we are to see those to whom we bring the Good News grow to maturity in Christ. When the Holy Spirit visits our hearts, we fall in love with God all over again. It is His unstoppable fire in our souls that is the catalyst for lasting transformation.

It is in relationship with the living God that the true and valid wellspring for missions comes from.

REFLECTION QUESTIONS

1. What does presenting everyone perfect in Christ mean to you?

_____

_____

_____

_____

_____

_____

_____

_____

_____
_____
_____
_____

2. What do you hope to gain from radical encounters with the Holy Spirit?

_____
_____
_____
_____
_____
_____
_____
_____
_____
_____
_____
_____
_____
_____
_____
_____

3. How do you feel about seeing great poverty and need in the midst of great spiritual transformation?

_____
_____
_____
_____
_____
_____
_____
_____
_____
_____
_____
_____
_____

SOUND DOCTRINE

"Remember your leaders, those who spoke to you the word of God.
Consider the outcome of their way of life and imitate their faith."
—HEBREWS 13:7

As Christians, we need sound doctrine that nourishes us, keeps our hearts set on God, and enables us to preach the full Gospel. Let's look first at the aspect of being nourished by doctrine.

"If you point these things out to the brothers, you will be a good minister of Christ Jesus, brought up in the truths of the faith and of the good teaching that you have followed" (1 Tim. 4:6). Sound doctrine is simply the truth about God, and only that truth will build us up in our faith. Thinking wrong things about God will weaken our faith and lead us away from Him. What we think about God affects how we feel about Him and all that we do. Good theology is used by the Holy Spirit to sustain revival, and bad theology is used by the enemy to destroy revival. Our mind and our hearts are connected, and sound doctrine is fundamentally concerned with matters of the heart. It protects our hearts from the ravages of "other gospels."

> *If anyone teaches false doctrines and does not agree to the sound instruction of our Lord Jesus Christ and to godly teaching, he is conceited and understands nothing. He has an unhealthy interest in controversies and quarrels about words…But godliness with contentment is great gain. For we brought nothing into the world, and we can take nothing out of it. …But you, man of God, flee from all this [unrighteousness], and pursue righteousness, godliness, faith, love, endurance and gentleness. Fight the good fight of the faith. Take hold of the eternal life to which you were called when you made your good confession in the presence of many witnesses. …In this way they will lay up treasure for themselves as a firm foundation for the coming age, so that they may take hold of the life that is truly life. …Turn away from godless chatter and the opposing ideas of what is falsely called knowledge, which some have professed and in so doing have wandered from the faith* (1 Timothy 6:3-4, 6-7, 11-12, 19–21).

"For the time will come when they will not endure sound doctrine; but wanting to have their ears tickled, they will accumulate for themselves teachers in accordance to their own desires" (2 Tim. 4:3 NASB).Paul was constantly concerned with protecting his sheep from false doctrine, and he did not hesitate to identify teachings that led astray. He did not shrink from controversy but boldly insisted on the truth, even at the expense of unity, if necessary. He had the purity of heart to do so in love with great fruit, always steering his flock away from anything that detracted from the power of the Cross.

REFLECTION QUESTIONS

1. How familiar are you with the doctrines of the Christian faith?

_____

_____

_____

_____

_____

_____

_____

_____

2. Do you think doctrine is important, or would you rather just "get out there and do the stuff"?

_____

_____

_____

_____

_____

_____

_____

_____

_____

3. Give some examples of doctrines of the faith that you think are necessary for a ministry like Iris or any mission-oriented ministry.

_____

_____

_____

_____

_____

_____

_____

_____

FRIENDSHIP WITH GOD

Heidi Baker

*"But as for me, the nearness of God is my good; I have made the
Lord God my refuge, that I may tell of all Your works."*
—Psalm 73:28 NASB

SESSION SUMMARY

There's something about hunger and thirst for the living God that brings Him, brings His manifest presence, in a way that nothing else can. I've noticed that wherever I go in the world, when people are truly hungry for God they can settle for nothing less. It becomes impossible to settle for less. They have such a hunger for God that can't stand to be left the same. I'm sure you've seen such people. They worship with abandon, take notes desperately trying to capture every word, every nuance of the Spirit, not wanting to miss a moment of His presence, hungry for God to crash in. Maybe you are one of those people!

Now is the time for you to allow God to shift you into His seamless river where the message and the worship become one. He wants to take you to that place where your heart is so fixed on Him that the worship and the word meld together in the burning fire of His presence until your heart is actually gilded to God. There are two definitions for the word *gild* that apply here. First, a guild is an association of people with similar interests. When your heart comes close to the heart of God, you can't help but share His interests. Second, when something is gilded it is covered with a thin layer of gold. God will gild your heart with His precious presence when you draw close. Let the Spirit quicken your heart to cleave closer and closer to God.

You have made known to me the path of life; You will fill me with joy in Your presence, with eternal pleasures at Your right hand (Psalm 16:11).

MAIN CONCEPTS FROM SESSION THREE

*"But as for me, the nearness of God is my good; I have made the
Lord God my refuge, that I may tell of all Your works."*
—Psalm 73:28 NASB

FRIENDSHIP WITH GOD

Heidi Baker

Spend Time with Jesus: *"May the God of hope fill you with all joy and peace as you trust in Him, so that you may overflow with hope by the power of the Holy Spirit."* —Romans 15:13

- Jesus always made time for God (see Luke 5:15-16).

- When we love Jesus, we will be purposeful about spending time with Him.

- With Jesus we can be the answer to someone's needs.

- Without Jesus we have nothing.

- The essence of missions: being the fragrance of Jesus to others.

To Be a Dependent People: *"How beautiful on the mountains are the feet of those who bring good news, who proclaim peace, who bring good tidings, who proclaim salvation, who say...'Your God reigns!'"* —Isaiah 52:7

- God is calling us to a life of total surrender.

- Face your own great poverty (see James 4:6).

- From a place of humility, He will lift you up (see James 4:10).

- Learn to receive Jesus. Know you are loved, cherished, kissed by the living God (see Eph. 1:15–19).

A Friend of God: *"I no longer call you servants, because a servant does not know his master's business. Instead, I have called you friends, for everything that I learned from My Father I have made known to you."* —John 15:15

- Become so intimate with God that He calls you "friend"—share in His secrets; learn His language; hear the deep things of His heart; share His heartaches and His joys.

- Listen to Jesus tell you who you are to Him and what you have access to through Him.

- Live with hands wide open to God.

- Give Him everything and He will give back what you need.

Because He Opened My Eyes: *"But where sin increased, grace increased all the more."* —Romans 5:20

- Don't be afraid to partake in God's suffering. He will walk you through it.

- God's perfect love will drive out fear and replace it with compassion.

- Reckless devotion to God sets up a mighty river of love that flows out of us and overtakes everything in its path.

No Longer Orphans: *"But You, O God, do see trouble and grief; You consider it to take it in hand. The victim commits himself to You; You are the helper of the fatherless."* —Psalm 10:14

- A spiritual orphan is anyone who is not connected to the Father.

- Jesus sends us to the lost in order to connect them to the Father, so that they will no longer be orphans.

- Step out of the "orphanage" and into the arms of God; then lead others there.

Come Away with God: *"My love calls to me: Arise, my darling. Come away, my beautiful one."* —Song of Solomon 2:10 HCSB

- Learn to live in a "come away" moment with God.

- Utterly abandon yourself to His affections in a heart-to-heart relationship.

- Receive God's best and then give it away!

Session Three Devotions

SPEND TIME WITH JESUS

"May the God of hope fill you with all joy and peace as you trust in Him, so that you may overflow with hope by the power of the Holy Spirit."
—ROMANS 15:13

I love to spend time with Jesus, to just simply adore Him. I love to pour my life out on Him like an alabaster box full of oil. Everything costly in my life I like to pour out on the One I love. He is so worthy! People often ask me how I live in this place of constantly pressing in for more, taking every opportunity to worship Jesus. Oftentimes it's not easy. Life, especially in Mozambique, is busy, noisy, hot, demanding, heartbreaking, and exhausting. I have learned that if my mind starts to wander, I pull it back to Jesus. I literally take authority over my wandering thoughts, and I give them to Jesus. I say, *"Jesus, I give You this time. I will worship You with everything within me. I will not be distracted. I will not be moved. This time belongs to You and I give it to You."* And then I abandon myself to Him and it becomes easy from there.

You will notice from the gospels that Jesus had to purposely make time for God. The crowds were constantly pressing in, wanting more of Him. In Jesus they found the manifest presence of God and they wanted more. They wanted His attention, they wanted His touch, they wanted to hear what He had to say; they wanted Him to heal them, to set them free. They couldn't get enough of Him. And Jesus couldn't get enough of His heavenly Father because He knew that His relationship with God was the place everything flowed from. *"Yet the news about Him spread all the more, so that crowds of people came to hear Him and to be healed of their sicknesses. But Jesus often withdrew to lonely places and prayed"* (Luke 5:15-16).

If I don't spend time with God, it becomes impossible for me to do what I do. Without Him I am small, weak, incapable, and ill-equipped. But when I allow myself to go and dwell in His presence, that's when His supernatural resources begin to flow into the situation. **With God I can be the answer to someone's need; without Him I am hopeless.** When we allow Jesus to express Himself through us, we become His hands and feet on the earth and that is the essence of missions—being the fragrance of Christ to others. When people see how much you trust God, they are more willing to trust Him.

REFLECTION QUESTIONS

1. What does your time with God look like?

_____

_____

_____

2. What are you willing to give up to spend time with God?

3. If your time alone with God is not yielding the kind of fruit you need or desire, what do you think is causing the blockage?

TO BE A DEPENDENT PEOPLE

"How beautiful on the mountains are the feet of those who bring good news, who proclaim peace, who bring good tidings, who proclaim salvation, who say…'Your God reigns!'"
—Isaiah 52:7

There is a mighty move of radical lovers of God who are being sent out to the ends of the earth! Are you ready to be one of these radical lovers, someone who will not be afraid to give away everything you have and go live among the poor? God longs to send you out to a people who are desperate for Him, who cannot live another day without Him. But you cannot be a sent out one unless you get into that place of total dependence on Him. He is calling you to an "I surrender all" kind of life. Today is the day!

In order to live a life of total surrender to God you must first become poor in spirit, facing your own great poverty with the understanding that *"God opposes the proud but gives grace to the humble"* (James 4:6). It is from that place of humility that we must learn to live. *"Humble yourselves before the Lord, and He will lift you up"* (James 4:10). We must receive before we can give. And what is it that God want us to receive? He wants us to understand who we are in Christ. He wants to firmly establish our identity in Christ. He wants us to receive Him.

What does it mean to receive God? It means we are sealed with the Holy Spirit who dwells in our hearts as a guarantee that God will fulfill His promises. As the people of God, we are marked with His Spirit (see 1 Pet. 2:10). **To receive God means that we know we are loved, cherished, kissed by the living God.** God wants to embrace you, to draw you so close that His very presence is like kisses to you. He wants you to feel His presence that comes from living in this place of His eternal embrace, this beatific vision, where you are so connected with Him that everything else no longer matters to you. God wants you to fall so in love with Him that anything He desires of you, you give to Him. He wants your time, your energy, your home, your possessions, your giftings, your life. It's quite simple really—God wants it all.

My prayers for you today are Paul's prayers for the Ephesians:

> *For this reason, ever since I heard about your faith in the Lord Jesus and your love for all the saints, I have not stopped giving thanks for you, remembering you in my prayers. I keep asking that the God of our Lord Jesus Christ, the glorious Father, may give you the Spirit of wisdom and revelation, so that you may know Him better. I pray also that the eyes of your heart may be enlightened in order that you may know the hope to which He has called you, the riches of His glorious inheritance in the saints, and His incomparably great power for us who believe* (Ephesians 1:15–19).

Amen!

REFLECTION QUESTIONS

1. How ready are you to become totally dependent on God, and what does that mean to you?

_____

_____

_____

_____

_____

_____

_____

2. How do you understand the aspect of being "poor in spirit"?

_____

_____

_____

_____

_____

_____

_____

3. How much are you in love with God right now?

_____

_____

_____

_____

_____

_____

_____

_____

A FRIEND OF GOD

"I no longer call you servants, because a servant does not know his master's business. Instead, I have called you friends, for everything that I learned from My Father I have made known to you."
—JOHN 15:15

I like to live life with my hands wide open, always laying it all down at the foot of the cross, giving everything to Him and allowing Him to choose what to pick up and put back in my hands. I want my life to be totally abandoned to the heart of the living God. Each day I say, *"Here it is God. Everything I have, everything I am, everything I will be, I lay it all down for You."* And once I've laid it all down, I ask Him for the Spirit of wisdom and revelation through Jesus Christ so that I might know Him better, know Him more fully. I want to be a friend of God, to know Him so fully and intimately that He calls me friend.

Do you want to be a friend of God, so close to Him that He actually shares His secrets with you? Do you want the kind of intimacy that goes beyond being an acquaintance? Are you hungry for all of God that you can get? That is how I live, with God as my friend, always hungry for Him. God is looking for friends. He wants to be closer to you. He wants to teach you His language. He wants to connect with you like a friend. God wants to share the deep things in His heart with you. He wants to talk to you about how He hears the children screaming, the three-year-olds who are being sold for sex. God wants to talk to you about how that feels for Him. He wants to talk to you about how He feels when people die because they don't have the simplest of medical care. He wants to talk to you about the brokenness of people. God wants to tell you His secrets about who you are and what you have access to. He wants to come closer to you than anyone in your life and whisper in your ears. He wants to be your friend. Are you ready?

Jesus lived with His hands wide open, always ready to give Himself away, ministering out of the fullness of His Father's presence. We can do the same. All we have to do is follow His example, sowing our lives into others. The overflow of His presence will give us what we need. There is such freedom in trusting God, such power. Let Him touch you with His love, compassion and tenderness. **Let each day find you hidden in the heart of Christ.**

"My grace is sufficient for you, for My power is made perfect in weakness." Therefore I will boast all the more gladly about my weakness, so that Christ's power may rest on me (2 Corinthians 12:9).

REFLECTION QUESTIONS

1. What do you have access to in your relationship with God?

_____
_____
_____
_____
_____
_____
_____

2. If you have "access" in your relationship with God, what are you doing with it? If you don't yet feel you have it, what would you do with it if you did?

_____
_____
_____
_____
_____
_____
_____
_____
_____
_____

3. How would you explain to someone the freedom that comes from trusting God using examples from your own life?

_____
_____
_____
_____
_____
_____
_____
_____
_____

BECAUSE HE OPENED MY EYES

"But where sin increased, grace increased all the more."
—ROMANS 5:20

The mission field is not an easy place to be. There is nothing glamorous about grinding poverty, the kind that wears people down until they have no hope. Holding dying people in your arms, seeing great need all around you and being able to do so little to alleviate the suffering of so many wears you down. But God is always there. I just get as close to Him as I can, then closer still, until I hear the whispers of His heart. **I refuse to give up because God doesn't give up.** I can't give up because He opened my eyes. Sometimes the pain of what He shows me is so overwhelming that everything in me wants to scream, *"Please, can I be blind again, just for one day? Please, could I not see for one day?"* But because God has won my heart and He's captured my affection, I cannot say I will be blind again. All I can do is what I am doing. I put my trust in Him.

Some people accuse God of not seeing, of not caring. "Why is there still suffering?" they ask. "Why is there still such intense poverty in the world? Is God sitting there with His arms folded? Is He somehow far away and far off and not concerned with abject poverty and abject pain and the depravity of man, of children being sold? Does He not hear the cry of the broken?" I know God hears the cry of the lost and broken because He sent us Jesus. He cares! God's heart is breaking too. He is standing before us now, extending His hand. All we have to do is reach out and take hold of His hand and be His friend. When we do, Jesus will walk with us and not overwhelm us. He will give you just enough for each day. Don't shut God out because the sounds of suffering are so hard to hear. Instead, allow Him to give you just enough to get through the minute, the hour, the day. Don't be afraid to partake in His suffering. He will walk you through it.

When you stop to reach out to just one person in need, you are reflecting the Father's heart. It is just that simple. His perfect love drives out fear and replaces it with compassion. Our reckless devotion to God sets up a mighty river of love that will flow out of us and over others, overtaking everything in its path. Are you ready to jump in the river?

REFLECTION QUESTIONS

1. How are you currently processing the great suffering you see around you in the mission field?

_____

_____

_____

_____

_____

2. If the idea of "jumping in the river" seems a bit scary, what specifically are you afraid of?

3. How does sharing God's great love help the poor?

NO LONGER ORPHANS

"But You, O God, do see trouble and grief; You consider it to take it in hand.
The victim commits himself to You; You are the helper of the fatherless."
—Psalm 10:14

It breaks God's heart when people don't know Him, when they are spiritually orphaned. **Every single person on the planet who hasn't been connected to the Father through Jesus is a spiritual orphan.** If you understand the reason that Jesus wants you to go and seek and find the lost, if you understand the lost as orphans—disconnected from family and true love, disconnected from God's care and His power and majesty, disconnected from their destinies—then you too will go. Not just to have them blurt out a sinner's prayer but to connect them to the Father so they too can be friends with God.

There's a difference between people who are paid to do a job and people who do it because of love. Friends do extraordinary things for each other, things that paid people never do. A friend gives everything needed without thinking twice. Friends don't think about giving a little percentage here, a little percentage there. True friends say, *"What I have is yours."* Do you know that God is the most amazing friend? He literally can do anything. He can open any door—in business, in ministry, in housing, in connections, in every way. That's the kind of friend God is.

Because He is omnipotent and omnipresent, God is actually able to be best friends with each one of us, all at the same time! But the deal is, it's mutual. If you don't give Him the time of day, don't trust Him, don't let Him in to the secrets of your heart, then you are hindering the two-way flow, the heart-to-heart relationship that He desires to have with you. Are you ready for friendship with God? Are you ready for the fact that friendship with Him is mutual? Are you ready to be friends with the perfect friend, the *only* perfect friend? Open up your heart and let Him in. He is waiting!

REFLECTION QUESTIONS

1. Have you personally experienced an orphan heart, and if so how did God heal your orphan heart?

_____

_____

_____

_____

_____

_____

_____

2. Take inventory of your friendship with God. Is your relationship with Him strong enough to enable His love to flow from you to those who don't know Him, to those who are not connected to Him?

3. What would it take for you to go deeper in your friendship with God?

COME AWAY WITH GOD

"My love calls to me: Arise, my darling. Come away, my beautiful one."
—Song of Solomon 2:10 HCSB

For years we lived in community on the mission field, in the slums, without much of anything; then God called us to Pemba. I remember hearing Him say, *"Come away, My beloved."* And I replied, "How am I going to come away, God? I have hundreds and hundreds of children. There are always eight or ten living with us. I don't understand 'come away.' What do You mean, 'come away'?" Then He said it again, *"Come away, My beloved. I want more time with you."* "Lord," I said. "You know what I'm doing, and I'm doing it for You. I don't understand come away." His answer was still, *"Come away, My beloved."* I kept asking and He kept saying, "come away" until it finally clicked. My son-in-law ended up writing a song in the midst of a mighty Holy Spirit moment all about coming away with God. I finally "got it." **He's so beautiful!** That's all that matters.

You see, when people are in love they give each other the best part of their day, the best time. They think about each other all the time. That's how I live with God. People are often confused at my behavior because they don't understand that I live in a "come away" moment so much of the time. I can't help it. I am so in love with God. He knows everything about me and He still wants to be close to me. He knows my failures, my weaknesses, the good, the bad, everything, and He still longs to draw me close. God knows the longings of my heart and the depth of my soul. I can't help but utterly abandon myself to His affections and His heart. It's the only place I want to be.

Because of this heart-to-heart relationship, I can never close my ears to the cries of the poor; I can never close my heart. God is my friend and I trust Him in all circumstances. I trust Him in the midst of the widows and orphans, with the dying and broken, with the lost, because He gave His best. He gave Jesus. Are you ready for God's best? Are you ready to come away with Him?

REFLECTION QUESTIONS

1. In the Gospel of Mark (Mark 6:31), Jesus and the disciples are tired and hungry in the midst of the crush of the crowds that have come to them. Jesus doesn't hesitate to draw away to a place of rest. How much are you able to draw away in the midst of great need going on around you?

_____

_____

_____

_____

_____

2. How do you explain the essence of drawing close to God versus just shutting out the world for a time?

3. How to you really feel about being closer to God? What would that look like for you?

Session Four

THE SOVEREIGNTY OF GOD

Rolland Baker

"Our God is in the heavens; He does all that He pleases."
—Psalm 115:3 ESV

SESSION SUMMARY

Heaven is a place of great joy because it is ruled by a God of great joy. As the people of God we should be running after the joy of the Lord instead of straightening our backs and bracing for a life of endurance. We are made in God's image and therefore we are made for joy. This joy of the Lord is not a fabricated, forced, fake emotion. It is not dependent on our circumstances. This kind of joy comes from living in the presence of our joyful God. How much fun it would be to live every minute of our lives lost in God's unlimited joy. But while the kingdom of God is about joy, it is also about balance. God desires that we find both joy and understanding in our relationship with Him. There is a time to be lost in joy and there is a time to think, to understand. God gives us freedom to flow back and forth between His joy and His understanding in the balance that comes from His perfection. When we find that place of balance, it steadies our feet and sets us on a more solid ground.

But just when we think we understand this concept of balance, God throws the fire of revival into our midst and sets up His sweet, holy chaos. Suddenly the ground under our feet isn't so steady anymore. Supernatural things start happening and no one really knows what is going on. Our tendency in the Church is to take revival in hand and tame it so that it won't get out of control! Our intentions are good—we don't want heresy, after all, and so God's revival is morphed into our agenda until the fire is brought under control. But thanks be to God that He doesn't stop at our efforts to control Him. He constantly brings His revival fire back to us because He is sovereign. His sovereignty brings freedom, which is perfect! He knows the desires of our hearts better than we do, for He created them. And He alone is able to satisfy them. Sovereignty does not mean forcing us to do what we don't want to do, but instead it changes our hearts so that we freely delight to do His will.

MAIN CONCEPTS FROM SESSION FOUR

"Our God is in the heavens; He does all that He pleases."
—Psalm 115:3 ESV

THE SOVEREIGNTY OF GOD

Rolland Baker

God Is Happy: *"The boundary lines have fallen for me in pleasant places; surely I have a delightful inheritance."* —Psalm 16:6

- God is happy, but we have a hard time being happy along with Him.

- We tend to let worry get in the way of joy.

- If we let go of control, trusting in God, it is easier to live in a place of joy.

Balance in the Kingdom: *"To a person who is good in His sight He has given wisdom and knowledge and joy."* —Ecclesiastes 2:26 NASB

- We need balance between joy and understanding in the Christian life.

- Too much theology can kill joy.

- Not enough theology puts us at risk.

- Freedom to flow between joy and wisdom is kingdom balance.

Sweet, Holy Chaos: *"The king's heart is in the hand of the Lord; He directs it like a watercourse wherever He pleases."* —Proverbs 21:1

- Revival is often messy—the wind of the Spirit blows where it will.

- Because things happen that we don't understand, we tend to want to control revival.

The Sovereignty of God: *"Humble yourselves, then, under God's mighty hand, so that He will lift you up in His own good time. Leave all your worries with Him, because He cares for you."* —1 Peter 5:6-7 GNT

- Lack of understanding about the sovereignty of God leads us to think that we know better than God what He wants and what He can and can't do.

- God is in charge, but He desires that we participate with Him.

- We kill missions and disable relationship with God when we think His sovereignty means that we have to do nothing.

Total Freedom: *"Now to Him who is able to keep you from stumbling, and to make you stand in the presence of His glory blameless with great joy, to the only God our Savior, through Jesus Christ our Lord, be glory, majesty, dominion and authority, before all time and now and forever. Amen."* —Jude 24-25 NASB

- Question: What is the sovereignty of God?

- Answer: God has the power to finish what He began in you and present you before the throne on that great day, blameless and spotless, without fault, with great joy in His presence.

- The sovereignty of God in you is energizing.

- His perfection working in you means you love what He loves—such freedom!

Session Four Devotions

GOD IS HAPPY

"The boundary lines have fallen for me in pleasant places;
surely I have a delightful inheritance."
—Psalm 16:6

There's no reason why you can't be having the greatest day of your life or the greatest moment of your life right now. Would you like to have that happen in the next two minutes? For most of us, as soon as our brain processes that question, we immediately begin to think about all the reasons why that can't happen. To begin with, there's too much to worry about, right? I mean, after all, we are responsible people. We're supposed to be on the lookout for problems and issues and then worry about them, right? Or are we?

When you stop to think about the reality of the Christian life, you realize that there is actually *nothing* to worry about, absolutely nothing, because God is in control. It's not up to us. We don't have to be responsible every waking moment of our lives because God is responsible. We can just *be* in the presence of God where there is fullness of joy. People think that preaching and teaching is all about helping others to overcome issues, learning how to be stronger, and all that sort of thing. But if we are full of the Holy Spirit we can give free rein to the Spirit and allow Him to fill us with the joy of the Lord. People who are full of the Spirit can't be depressed no matter how hard they try. The two just don't go together.

There was a time when I was very apologetic about having so much fun all the time. I would hear comments like, "Humor has no place in the church," or "Get serious!" Do you realize that God is happier than you are? He's more childlike than you and He has way more fun than you too. Think for a moment about children when they play. When a child is happy and playing, do you think they're justifying their joy and trying to figure out on what grounds they should be behaving that way? Of course not. And it's the same with God. He's just happy. He's just fun! How do I know this? Because our kids in Mozambique, especially in the early years, have been to the throne room of God and they will tell you that it's not a place where everybody is just solemnly bowing for a thousand years. It's a place of great joy! Jesus went to the cross because He knew about this joy. He knew what was in store for you and me. He's there now in the midst of this joy, and He's inviting you to join in. Isn't it time to accept His invitation?

REFLECTION QUESTIONS

1. When you think about the possibility of having the greatest moment of your life right now, what could stop that from happening?

_____

_____

_____

_____

_____

_____

_____

_____

2. What is it about responsibility that blocks your joy?

_____

_____

_____

_____

_____

_____

_____

_____

3. What do you make of the idea that God is happy?

_____

_____

_____

_____

_____

_____

_____

_____

BALANCE IN THE KINGDOM

"To a person who is good in His sight He has given wisdom and knowledge and joy."
—Ecclesiastes 2:26 NASB

Theology has a strong tendency to be a joy killer if you don't understand its true content. Theology is simply whatever you think about God, your attitude is toward God. Everyone has theology. If you're groaning inwardly right now and thinking, *"Oh no, not another class on theology! I just want to get on with it,"* you have actually just expressed your theology. Let's face it, when we have to think and process how we feel and why we feel the way we do, it can end up being a huge struggle. Understanding often doesn't come without struggle, and we certainly need understanding, so we struggle.

But you're saying, "Wait, Rolland. You just told us not to struggle and worry; just to be happy." Well, yes I did, but now I'm telling you that we need joy *and* understanding in the Christian life. There is no one way of looking at everything. **We need multiple perspectives in the Christian life in order to love one another and go forward to what lies ahead.** We need balance in the kingdom of God. How you interpret what is going on depends on what perspective you're coming from. I'm not talking about discerning apostate theology. I'm talking about finding that place of balance between abandoned joy and understanding. Is God in control, or are you doing what you want to do? It depends on how you look at it. Should you think hard to understand God, or should you just be a kid and not worry about it? It depends on how you look at it.

Paul said to Timothy, *"Think over what I say, for the Lord will give you understanding in everything"* (2 Tim. 2:7 ESV), but Psalm 131 says not to concern ourselves with great matters but to quiet ourselves like babies. Which is it? Well, sometimes it feels really good to think and other times it doesn't; we just want to chill. That's the perfection of the kingdom. What if you had to think hard all the time just to stay afloat? Or, what if you were not allowed to think, if you were just told to "follow." Neither of those is good. We need balance. We need the freedom to flow from joy to understanding and back. *"Happy is a man who finds wisdom, and who acquires understanding"* (Prov. 3:13 HCSB). God is perfection, and He wants us to learn to live in the balance that comes from His perfection. If you're looking for a good kingdom, this is it—God's kingdom is the best!

REFLECTION QUESTIONS

1. Take some time to think through your own theology and then sum it up as best you can in a paragraph or two.

_____

_____

_____

_____

_____

_____

_____

_____

_____

_____

_____

2. Where do you tend to camp out, in joy or understanding? Why do you think that is?

_____

_____

_____

_____

_____

_____

_____

_____

_____

_____

_____

_____

3. What would it take for you to get into a comfortable place of balance in your life between joy and understanding, and what does "comfortable" mean to you in this equation?

_____

_____

_____

_____

_____

_____

_____

_____

_____

_____

SWEET, HOLY CHAOS

*"The king's heart is in the hand of the Lord; He directs it
like a watercourse wherever He pleases."*
—PROVERBS 21:1

People try hard to understand what is going on when a mighty move of the Spirit hits somewhere in the world. And then you come to places like Harvest School where it is expected that we will explain things, make things clear, give understanding, but who can understand the things of the Spirit? The wind of the Spirit comes and it goes and you don't know where it's coming or going, but you sure know when you have it! We shouldn't live life simply according to principles and techniques because the Holy Spirit isn't either of these. He is a living person who's moving inside of us, and when **God moves things can sometimes get wild and crazy and amazing.** That's what happens in revival. Revival hits and supernatural things start happening and people begin to experience God in ways they don't understand. It's quite amazing, but our human nature doesn't always see God as amazing. We want to control Him instead of being amazed by Him. When God brings revival we start asking, "Who's in charge? Where do we meet? What do we do?" When the Holy Spirit hits, we know something is happening and that it's really exciting. We want to be a part of what God is doing, but we don't know how to just let God be God.

Instead, our human nature kicks in. Leaders pop up to help organize and get people to meet at the *right* time and do things together and believe the *right* things and be protected from error and make sure the Holy Spirit is pastored. The implication is that if the Holy Spirit were as mature as a pastor, we could let Him out safely, but until then we need rules. Yes, our rules help us to get organized so that we can cooperate and do bigger things than we can separately, and sometimes this is true. And we do need to weed out obvious heresy and all the other problems that can come with revival, but when we start trying to control God's presence and power, we end up injecting our own agendas and desire into the situation until everything is "under control." With all this control, the fire begins to diminish. This is what we do to revival until God comes along again and throws a glory bomb somewhere on the planet and revival breaks out afresh and the cycle repeats itself. What will it take for us to receive the sweet holy chaos of God's revival and not put it out because we want control?

REFLECTION QUESTIONS

1. How comfortable or uncomfortable are you when God's sweet, holy chaos hits?

_____

_____

_____

_____

_____
_____
_____
_____
_____
_____
_____
_____

2. Do you believe there should be any sort of structure in the midst of a mighty move of God and, if so, what should it look like?

_____
_____
_____
_____
_____
_____
_____
_____
_____
_____
_____
_____
_____

3. Aside from the reasons given here, what do you think we are really trying to control in revival and why?

_____
_____
_____
_____
_____
_____
_____
_____
_____
_____
_____
_____

THE SOVEREIGNTY OF GOD

"Humble yourselves, then, under God's mighty hand, so that He will lift you up in His own good time. Leave all your worries with Him, because He cares for you."
—1 Peter 5:6-7 GNT

The sovereignty of God tends to be a difficult thing for people to wrap their minds around. The usual reaction to the issue of the sovereignty of God is, "Well, if God is in control and He runs everything and decides everything, and it's not up to me, where is my motivation to do anything?" People tend to stay away from the issue of sovereignty because it kills missions. Sovereignty as most people understand it puts the brakes on a relationship with God unless we approach it from the opposite direction. Think about this—would you be motivated to give your life away to a God who is out of control, a God who doesn't have power, who can't determine things, a God who isn't safe to trust? Let's say you're going along in life not knowing what the best thing for your life is, but God doesn't know either so you have to tell Him. And He's just waiting for you to learn how to properly pray and figure things out. And all of heaven is waiting on the edge of their seats to see what you're going to do next because they have no idea what's coming and neither does God.

Why, if God were even slightly out of control, how would we sleep at night? If He were not omnipotent, would you trust your entire life to Him for all eternity? What if it were all up to you now? If you're the weakest link in the chain, guess where things break? Lots of people make statements such as, "Oh, God doesn't send people to hell; God didn't do that." There is a lot of talk about what God can and can't do, what God does and doesn't do, as if it's not up to God. I hear people say, "God's just waiting, waiting on you. He's practically screaming at you, but you're not listening. God is trying, but you won't cooperate. He's so frustrated because people aren't responding to Him." That kind of theology is very prevalent. My response to all of this is, "If you don't like the idea of God's sovereignty, try something else and see how that works for you."

What does sovereignty really mean? Well, we're talking about a perfect God. We're not talking about a Hitler who has all power. We're not talking about a human being who has all power. We're talking about God who has all power, and that turns sovereignty into something completely different. We have a God who gives life through His sovereignty. He doesn't shut us down and restrict us and make us feel chained and bound. He's a life-giver. Jesus said, *"I came that you might have life, and have it more abundantly."* Well, how is He going to do that if He's not in control?

REFLECTION QUESTIONS

1. What is your current understanding of God's sovereignty?

_____

_____

_____
_____
_____
_____
_____
_____
_____
_____

2. How would you explain to someone that God gives life through His sovereignty?

_____
_____
_____
_____
_____
_____
_____
_____
_____
_____
_____

3. When you see things around you that are deeply heartbreaking, do you _inwardly_ question God's sovereignty?

_____
_____
_____
_____
_____
_____
_____
_____
_____

TOTAL FREEDOM

"Now to Him who is able to keep you from stumbling, and to make you stand in the presence of His glory blameless with great joy, to the only God our Savior, through Jesus Christ our Lord, be glory, majesty, dominion and authority, before all time and now and forever. Amen."
—Jude 24-25 NASB

What does sovereignty really mean? I believe sovereignty means God has the power to finish what He began in you and present you before the throne on that great day, blameless and spotless, without fault and with great joy in His presence. That's what He is able to do. Hallelujah! And if He is really at work in you, why would you not run the race, make every effort, strive in every way possible, love God with all your strength because you *want* to, because you know you have a powerful God who is able to make that happen in you?

A sovereign God means that if you have a desire for God, He is at work in you. And when you get to know Him, you realize that your experience of His sovereignty is total freedom. And if He is not at work in you, you don't have freedom because you're fighting your own conscience all the time; you're fighting your own weaknesses all the time. Isn't it exhilarating to think that because you know that God is all-powerful, you love that about Him? And because you love that about Him, you want to confirm His calling in everything you do. The last thing you'd want to do is refuse His work in you. The last thing you'd want to do is become passive and think, "Oh, it's just God's job."

The sovereignty of God gives me energy because I realize He is absolutely in control of everything about me. Knowing He's a perfect God means that I *want* to go with Him. The perfection of God is that He is able to go out of Himself and put into you and me a love for what He loves. **The more you voluntarily love what God loves, the more free and satisfying your relationship is with Him because you will live in a place of trusting Him constantly to work out His plans in your life.**

I don't know how our churches in the bush have hung together all these years. They don't have email, texts or phones. We see these churches and their leaders maybe once a year, if that. This whole group of churches is so supernatural we can't explain it. People want to know how to replicate what we do here and the answer is, "We have no idea." It's the sovereignty of God working through all of us.

> *But whenever anyone turns to the Lord, the veil is taken away. Now the Lord is the Spirit, and where the Spirit of the Lord is, there is freedom. And we, who with unveiled faces all reflect the Lord's glory, are being transformed into His likeness with ever-increasing glory, which comes from the Lord, who is the Spirit* (2 Corinthians 3:16–18).

REFLECTION QUESTIONS

1. Take time to reflect on how much freedom you are experiencing in your life and your relationship with God right now.

2. Does the sovereignty of God energize you? Confuse you? How does it make you feel?

3. Reflect on some of the ways in which you see God going out of Himself and putting into you a love for what He loves. How are you responding to this?

Part Two

WHO YOU ARE

Session Five

IDENTITY

Heidi Baker

*"Yet to all who received Him, to those who believed in His
name, He gave the right to become children of God."*
—John 1:12

SESSION SUMMARY

In 1996, I was a burned-out missionary ready to walk off the mission field and go work at Kmart. Rolland and I had spent years in Asia and Europe and a year in Mozambique ministering to the poor and lost, and I was tremendously weary from trying to give out of my own strength. I didn't fully understand who I was in God's heart. Thankfully, God in His great love profoundly touched my life at a conference in Toronto, Canada and began to teach me about my true identity. Randy Clark was preaching that day and spoke a word from God over me. "God wants to know, do you want the nation of Mozambique?" he cried out. My heart responded with a resounding "Yes!" Struck by the presence of almighty God, for seven days and seven nights I was rendered completely helpless so that He could get my full attention and speak directly to my heart. Unable to walk, talk, or do anything for myself, I simply lay on the floor of the church in God's presence. I was carried to a car at night dropped off on the bed in my hotel room. In the morning four people came back to carry me to the car and take me back to the church. Gently, He took me up and into His heart, directing me to the Book of Ephesians. With a great deal of effort, I was finally able to speak the word "Ephesians" to Rolland who began to read it to me. For days he read to me, over and over until the words of Paul's letter were burning inside of me with a holy fire of radical love, transforming my identity. My time on the floor with God in Toronto was only the beginning though. From that place of surrender I have been learning to live in God's great love that is always on full display if you have the eyes to see it.

Since our time in Mozambique, God has continued to teach us about the fullness of our identity. I have come to appreciate that each one of us has a unique identity given to us by the Father, so that together the "sum of the parts" brings the wholeness of His presence to us individually and corporately. **I now know what it is to be so free that I'm not afraid to receive blessings—so free that I can live in the darkest slum with great joy because God is there with me.** Like Jesus, I can give myself away fearlessly because of who God is. I have come to understand that my identity is not found in what I do but in who I am in Christ. Because I know this truth, I can say "Yes" to Him always and everywhere.

MAIN CONCEPTS FROM SESSION FIVE

*"Yet to all who received Him, to those who believed in His
name, He gave the right to become children of God."*
—JOHN 1:12

IDENTITY

Heidi Baker

Knowing Who You Are: *"Praise be to the God and Father of our Lord Jesus Christ, who has blessed us in the heavenly realms with every spiritual blessing in Christ."* —Ephesians 1:3

- As individuals, we can do nothing without God and the Church.

- The Book of Ephesians gives us fuller understanding of God's purpose for the Church.

- Through our union with Christ, as His bride, we can receive every spiritual blessing.

Step Into Your God-Given Identity: *"Since we have gifts that differ according to the grace given to us, each of us is to exercise them accordingly."* —Romans 12:6 NASB

- God loves you! God adores you! God has a calling for you.

- You are unique, and your unique calling is an important part of the body of Christ.

- Don't try to copy someone else's calling—it doesn't work.

- When you walk in your own calling, you come alive.

Enjoy the Cheese: *"I am not saying this because I am in need, for I have learned to be content whatever the circumstances."* —Philippians 4:11

- Honor those who honor you.

- Learn to love yourself in the midst of sacrifice.

- Learn how to be free enough in Christ to receive the blessings others offer you.

Receive Your Inheritance: *"I will not leave you as orphans; I will come to you."* —John 14:18

- As God's beloved child, you have a heavenly Father who always loves you and will always provide for you.

- Because of the precious Holy Spirit, we can live as children of God with all His blessings.

- Childlike faith enables us to embrace God's love for us.

True Freedom: *"For I resolved to know nothing while I was with you except Jesus Christ and him crucified."* —1 Corinthians 2:2

- True freedom in the Christian life comes from total dependence on God.

- Jesus modeled this kind of freedom for us in His birth, life, and death.

- Great need on the mission field provides great opportunity for God.

- Study the life of Jesus to learn how to be a missionary.

- When people see how great God is, they get excited about giving their life to Him.

Session Five Devotions

KNOWING WHO YOU ARE

"Praise be to the God and Father of our Lord Jesus Christ, who has blessed
us in the heavenly realms with every spiritual blessing in Christ."
—Ephesians 1:3

I love the Book of Ephesians, and I love that God made it come alive to me in such a supernatural way in Toronto. Paul's purpose in writing this letter to the church in Ephesus was to bring them a fuller understanding of God's eternal purpose for both the Church as a whole and each one of us as members of the body of Christ. Paul opens his letter with what scholars refer to as a "doxology," which is another word for a literary form used to praise God. In the original Greek, Ephesians 1:3–14 was one long sentence. It has since been broken up into three distinct sections to illustrate the blessings we have through the Trinity. Verse 3 tells us of the blessings we have through the Father, verses 4–13 tell us of our blessings through the Son, and 13-14 tell us of the blessings the Holy Spirit has for us.

As I lay on the floor in Toronto, Jesus spoke to me. He said, **"You can do nothing without Me, and nothing without the body of Christ."** What a revelation that was! Like many who go into the mission field, I had this burning desire to rock the world for Jesus. I wanted to change this planet and see the love of Christ burst forth and the power of God pour out and change everything. I kept charging out there under my own strength only to find that I constantly ran out of strength. I didn't know that before we can understand what God wants us to do or where He wants us to go, we need to step into this place of who we are in His heart. It was not until God took me up into His heart where I was literally incapacitated with the holy, heavy-weighted glory of Him that I could begin to understand what He was saying to me.

Through our union with our risen Lord Jesus we receive *every* spiritual blessing in the heavenly realms. This is true for us as individuals and as the Church. We have been chosen—divinely elected! We are precious sons and daughters of the Most High God! What an inheritance! What an identity!

REFLECTION QUESTIONS

1. What is your understanding of God's eternal purpose for the Church? For you?

_____

_____

_____

_____

_____

2. What do you mean when you talk about union with the risen Lord Jesus?

_____

3. How do you define "every spiritual blessing in the heavenly realms"?

_____

STEP INTO YOUR GOD-GIVEN IDENTITY

"Since we have gifts that differ according to the grace given
to us, each of us is to exercise them accordingly."
—Romans 12:6 NASB

Do you know that your heavenly Father absolutely adores you? He looks at you and says, "You're My favorite." It's true! God actually looks at you and He loves you. The fullness of this revelation is glorious. Each one of us is unique. God has a destiny designed specifically for you. When you try to copy someone else's destiny it doesn't work, but when you step into who you are in God you come alive!

Rolland loves theology. He will sit and talk for hours about the richness of the depths of God. Some of you may think that to be a missionary you always have to be out there "doing" instead of sitting talking theology. **But the truth is that God made each one of us with different gifts according to the grace given to us, and He wants us to exercise them accordingly**. We need to get rid of our own notions of what it means to be a missionary and learn to embrace God's holy destiny for our lives because that's when we can truly become "sent out ones." Does Rolland do nothing but sit around talking theology? Of course not. But it is an integral part of who he is, and he delights in this and every aspect of his God-given identity.

People are always asking us what our plan is—what's our five-year plan, our ten-year plan? I tell them my plan is to love God with all my heart, mind, soul, and spirit, and to love my neighbor as myself. That's my plan because it is Jesus' plan. When I find my identity in Him, His plan becomes my plan. It's just that simple. God wants you to understand who He created you to be and to delight yourself in Him: *"Delight yourself in the Lord and he will give you the desires of your heart"* (Ps. 37:4). What are the desires of your heart? When you come into your identity in Christ, the desires of His heart become the desires of your heart.

REFLECTION QUESTIONS

1. How do you feel about the revelation that God adores you?

---

2. What are your God-given gifts?

3. What do you think it means to be a missionary, and how is God changing this perception?

ENJOY THE CHEESE

"I am not saying this because I am in need, for I have learned
to be content whatever the circumstances."
—PHILIPPIANS 4:11

Sacrifice has always been something that's a delight to Rolland and me. We have given away everything we've owned several times. It has been easy for us to give and go, give and go, but for years I couldn't understand the "love yourself" part of being a missionary. I thought being sold out and radical for Jesus meant total self-sacrifice without understanding the blessings. I didn't know it, but I was afraid to receive. In an effort to be the best missionary on earth I thought I had to reject anything that didn't look like total sacrifice. I would look at the generations of missionaries in Rolland's family and think that my first-generation missionary self could only catch up through neglecting to receive any material blessings. I wasn't free enough in Christ to receive the blessings others offered to me.

As Rolland and I began to travel the world sharing our experiences in the mission field, our hosts, if they were able, would bless us with lovely accommodations, often complete with baskets of delicious foods such as fresh fruit and cheese. I would walk into our hotel room and look at the big soaking tub in the bathroom and the scrumptious food and think to myself, "I'm not eating that cheese! We're missionaries. We live among the poor who will never eat cheese. And I'm not soaking in that big tub of warm water. There is no such thing on the mission field. What decadence! These things are unfit for *real* missionaries!" It wasn't until God pinned me to the floor in Toronto and said, "Heidi, eat cheese and take a hot bath," that I began to understand. There's something about this realm where you find out who you are and you find out God's okay with you receiving blessings, and you're okay with it too. You're okay with whatever situation you're in when you know who you are. There's something that happens when your identity shifts. You're so free that you're not afraid to suffer, so free that you're not afraid to be blessed. God really worked on my heart. He showed me that I was dishonoring the people who were trying to honor me.

There was a time when I would get physically ill when I would go to a restaurant that had a lot of food. Buffets would make me ill. I would think of the poor and hungry who were so close to my heart and I couldn't enjoy the food. When I think back to some of the things I did, I'm embarrassed, but I want to share my struggles because I know they are common to many who go into missions. Like me, you may have "trouble with the cheese," but when you submit your heart to God, He will shift it. Now I'm good with whatever is provided for me. I can sleep in a five-star hotel or on a rope bed with three children and a chicken (although honestly I don't really sleep when I'm in a crowded rope bed). The point is, I am content because I know who I am.

REFLECTION QUESTIONS

1. What does sacrifice on the mission field mean to you?

_____

_____

_____

_____

_____

_____

_____

2. What shifting needs to take place in your heart right now?

_____

_____

_____

_____

_____

_____

_____

3. In Philippians 4:11, what is Paul saying and how does that translate for the mission field?

_____

_____

_____

_____

_____

_____

_____

RECEIVE YOUR INHERITANCE

"I will not leave you as orphans; I will come to you."
—John 14:18

The children we work with in Mozambique are true orphans in every sense of the word when they first come to us—until God's love overtakes them. Then them become sons and daughters. It is amazing to see how easy it is for them to embrace their new identity in Christ once they "get it." I think we learn more from the children than they learn from us because their hearts are so open to believe and receive all that Father God has for them. This is true for a lot of the Mozambique adults too. They constantly demonstrate a childlike faith that we in the West find hard to grasp.

One of our older girls—a sweet, beautiful child—had a dream to go to America and study but needed a scholarship. I was talking with one of the "mammas" who oversee the house where this dear girl lives and I said, "Let's believe that I'm going to find a scholarship for her." A few days later in our staff meeting, this mamma told me, ""Mamma, you don't need to find a scholarship. We already found one." They called her the night before. She received a full scholarship. **It takes a childlike faith to move from the orphanage to the family house**. This is what life looks like when we understand our identity. We are no longer orphans without a father to care for us. We know who our heavenly Father is and that He always provides.

We constantly tell our children that they are not orphans, and I want to say to you right now, "You are not an orphan. You are loved by God." He wants to take you into the spiritual realms with Him where you're so free that all things are possible because of Jesus. He is inviting you to take your place as sons and daughters in His house. When Jesus says to His disciples, *"I will not leave you as orphans; I will come to you,"* He is talking about two things. He is talking about the Holy Spirit who is available to all who believe and about His second coming. We are living right now in the time of the Holy Spirit, the Counselor, the Spirit of Truth who Jesus says will be with us forever. In John 14:23, Jesus says, *"If anyone loves me, he will obey my teaching. My Father will love him, and we will come to him and make our home with him."* Jesus has flung open the doors to God's house and invited us in. Step through the door! Receive your inheritance! Then you can go anywhere God sends you. You can go high, you can go low, you can speak to presidents and kings because you live in the heavenly realms where God blesses you with every spiritual blessing.

REFLECTION QUESTIONS

1. In John 14, Jesus explains to the disciples why He must go to the Father, and then He tells them about the promised Holy Spirit. How much is the precious Holy Spirit a part of your life?

_____

_____

_____

_____

_____

_____

_____

2. What does it take for you to leave the last of your baggage behind in the "orphanage" and move into God's house?

_____

_____

_____

_____

_____

_____

_____

_____

_____

_____

3. Jesus talks often about the importance of becoming like little children. If you struggle with the idea of childlike faith, what is at the root of your struggle?

_____

_____

_____

_____

_____

_____

_____

_____

TRUE FREEDOM

"For I resolved to know nothing while I was with you
except Jesus Christ and him crucified."
—1 Corinthians 2:2

We often overlook one of the foundational aspects of how Jesus operated in total freedom while here on earth. For Jesus, it was about dependence. He was born in the flesh—a tiny, naked, totally dependent baby. He had to learn to crawl in the dirt before he could walk. He had to learn to speak a language. Why did God have Jesus come to us in this way? I believe He wanted to teach us about dependence, about love, connection, and family, and He did this through the life of His Son. He wanted us to see what it was like to empty ourselves and become totally dependent on Him, totally dependent on the empowering of the Holy Spirit. This is how Jesus was born, grew up, and lived His life. If you want to know how to do missions, look at Jesus. Study Jesus. Look at the way He humbled himself, the way He poured Himself out. He was not afraid to be born in a stable. He could have been born anywhere, but He chose dependence and out of that dependence came the freedom to lay His life down.

God is calling you to total dependence so that you can live in total freedom. He isn't looking for people who just listen to a message or adhere to commandments. God is looking for radical lovers who will hold fast to the person of Jesus Christ because they understand that no force of violence could take His life from Him because He gave it freely. God is looking for people who will surrender everything to make room for the precious Holy Spirit who brings the only authentic freedom to be found. This kind of attachment to the person and perspective of Jesus Christ must be our goal, especially in the mission field, lest we look at the great need in front of us and think that is our mission.

When Rolland and I first came to Mozambique and saw the overwhelming need, we rejoiced because we knew that we were powerless to accomplish anything, and for that reason God would receive all the glory. This is how the kingdom comes in the mission field—in God's power alone. Your identity is never in what you do; it's in who you are in Christ. Find your joy in being His! Get excited about giving away the greatest treasure on earth for free and know true freedom!

REFLECTION QUESTIONS

1. How much are you able to live in freedom while totally depending on God?

----

2. What does it mean to attach yourself to the person and perspective of Jesus?

3. In First Corinthians 2 Paul talks about coming in weakness and fear rather than with eloquence or wisdom as he proclaimed the testimony of God. What is he saying and why is it important in the mission field?

Session Six

IDENTITY AND INDIVIDUALITY

Heidi Baker

"What is more, I consider everything a loss compared to the surpassing greatness of knowing Christ Jesus my Lord, for whose sake I have lost all things."
—Philippians 3:8

SESSION SUMMARY

Within days of our wedding, Rolland and I headed into the mission field. We were young and full of hope and zeal and expectation. We loved the Lord deeply, and it was the greatest desire of our hearts to serve Him with every fiber of our being. We headed off to Indonesia to change the world for Jesus. In those early years, we gave it everything we had. We poured ourselves out until there was virtually nothing left. It was when my inner resources ran dry and I was feeling strongly like giving up that things began to change. I came to the end of myself and the beginning of a whole new relationship with God. He rendered me helpless so that I could understand who He is and how much He loves me. **While we thought we were going to change the world for Jesus, He changed us for the world.**

We became radical lovers when God revealed to us the depths of His radical love in Jesus. We died to self again and again, going lower and then lower still. When everything around us screamed "impossible," God showed us that everything is possible with Him. We learned what it means to give your life away with great joy and peace because God is in charge. Our orphan spirits gave way to His Spirit of adoption. We stood on His feet and held His hands daily in the midst of impossible odds as He revealed His glory all around us. We learned how to allow the Master Artist to paint on the canvas of our lives in order to reveal His beauty. I can't wait to wake up in the morning and soak again in God's presence, to pray and worship with His family, to let Him fully possess me all over again. Nothing compares to those times when I can abandon myself into the Father's arms like a child, totally in love with God. Following God is my greatest joy. I want nothing more than to be His.

MAIN CONCEPTS FROM SESSION SIX

"What is more, I consider everything a loss compared to the surpassing greatness of knowing Christ Jesus my Lord, for whose sake I have lost all things."
—PHILIPPIANS 3:8

IDENTITY AND INDIVIDUALITY

Heidi Baker

Radical Lovers: *"Truly, truly, I say to you, unless a grain of wheat falls into the earth and dies, it remains alone: but if it dies, it bears much fruit."* —John 12:24 NASB

- The reality of death on the mission field means dying to self, becoming alive in Christ.

- Radical lovers understand God's radical love for all, are fully filled with the Holy Spirit, are possessed by the living God, are so yielded that God is able to move freely through them.

I Can't, but God Can: *"In Him we were also chosen, having been predestined according to the plan of Him who works out everything in conformity with the purpose of His will, in order that we, who were the first to hope in Christ, might be for the praise of His glory."* —Ephesians 1:11-12

- God works out *all* things according to His purposes.

- Empty yourself to make room for God.

- God living in you can do all things.

- Give your life away with great peace and joy because God is in charge.

- God's power is made perfect in our weakness.

The DNA of Father God: *"And surely I am with you always, to the very end of the age."* —Matthew 28:20

- We carry God's DNA with us wherever we go.

- We have a safe and secure place in God's heart.

- In God's heart we will find affirmation, protection, and true identity.

- God makes us feel powerful when we surrender to His power and love.

- God lives in us through Jesus; therefore, we are never orphans.

Step Into Your Calling: *"For we are His workmanship, created in Christ Jesus for good works, which God prepared beforehand so that we would walk in them."* —Ephesians 2:10 NASB

- We often make "wrong turns" before we find God's path to our calling.

- As your relationship with God grows deeper, you are better able to understand His plans for you.

- Press into God; step into your calling.

You Are God's Possession: *"And you also were included in Christ when you heard the word of truth, the gospel of your salvation. Having believed, you were marked in Him with a seal, the promised Holy Spirit, who is a deposit guaranteeing our inheritance until the redemption of those who are God's possession—to the praise of His glory."* —Ephesians 1:13-14

- Give yourself fully to God.

- Become His possession; carry His glory.

- Let possession become your lifestyle.

- Each one of us is a beautiful painting from the hand of God.

- We can pick up the paintbrush and mess up the painting, but when we hand the brush back to God, He will make us beautiful again.

Session Six Devotions

RADICAL LOVERS

*"Truly, truly, I say to you, unless a grain of wheat falls into the earth
and dies, it remains alone: but if it dies, it bears much fruit."*
—John 12:24 NASB

During the years we have been in the mission field, Rolland and I have faced death many times. We have been imprisoned, shipwrecked, robbed, mugged, assaulted by all manner of diseases, received death threats, stood at gun point and knife point, faced armed extortion, and been assailed by angry mobs. Both of us have recovered from what the doctors termed incurable diseases. We have faced riots, accusations of drug trafficking and trafficking in human body parts, and the list goes on. The mission field is not a safe place in the natural. The possibility of dying for your faith is a reality for missionaries. People die for their faith every day in the mission field. Some are ready to die; some are not. But how does one "get ready"? It begins with knowing who you are in Christ. When you understand God's radical love for you in Jesus, you're able to become a radical lover too. Radical lovers of Jesus aren't afraid to die for Him because they have already died to self. When you reflect on John 12:24, it becomes obvious that in order to be fruitful for the kingdom the "old man" must be put to death so that one can become "new" in Christ.

Many of you are eager to become the most radical lovers who ever hit the earth because you have come to understand God's great love in Jesus as expressed in John 3:16: *"For God so loved the world that he gave his only begotten Son."* You have received such a profound revelation of what Jesus did for you on the cross that *all* of your life is becoming radically connected to God. You no longer have to try and be someone other than who God made you to be. You have stepped into the destiny He has for you, fully filled with the Holy Spirit and possessed by the living God, so yielded that He is able to move freely through your unique personality to do His will. **Radical lovers see the power of God and receive more than they could ask or imagine because God pours out His Spirit without measure on those who love Him with abandon**. Radical lovers filled with the Spirit can do more in one day than we could do in the flesh in a thousand years. Second Chronicles 16:9 says, *"For the eyes of the Lord range throughout the earth to strengthen those whose hearts are fully committed to him."* Are you ready to fearlessly give your heart fully to Him, to give your life fully to Him? He is waiting for you to say "Yes!"

REFLECTION QUESTIONS

1. Jesus often taught in metaphors like the one He used in John 12:24, but the reality of death in the mission field is not metaphorical; it is very real. How do we deal with this reality?

_____

_____

_____

_____

_____

_____

_____

_____

_____

_____

_____

_____

_____

2. Spend time today reflecting deeply on God's radical gift of His Son and then write down what the Holy Spirit is saying to you. How do you think God wants you to use these particular Holy Spirit revelations?

_____

_____

_____

_____

_____

_____

_____

_____

_____

_____

_____

I CAN'T, BUT GOD CAN

"In him we were also chosen, having been predestined according to the plan of him who works out everything in conformity with the purpose of his will, in order that we, who were the first to hope in Christ, might be for the praise of his glory."
—Ephesians 1:11-12

What if you actually believed that the words of Ephesians 1:11-12 were true? Think on that for a moment. If you really believe God works out absolutely *everything—every single last thing*—in conformity with the purpose of His will, would you live your life with total abandon to Him? When you really understand who God is, and who you are, and who Jesus is, and what it means for you to work with Father, Son, and Holy Spirit as a participant in the Divine Nature, would you no longer be afraid to empty yourself and become nothing? The apostle Paul put it this way in Philippians 2:6-7: *"Who, being in very nature God, did not consider equality with God something to be grasped, but made himself nothing, taking the very nature of a servant."* The Greek word for this is *kenosis*, which means the self-emptying of one's own will in order to become entirely receptive to God's divine will.

I like to reflect that when I empty myself I've made room for God to fill me up with Himself. It's so beautiful when that happens. Our true character is able to come out when we allow God to fill us. Every one of us has a way of presenting who God is through our own particular life. We become alive in Christ, the living word of God, radiating who He is. You may be the only Bible some people will ever "read." They will "read" the word of God in your life because they are able to see what love looks like when they look at you.

Make no mistake; you will be challenged, daily. God will tell you to do something and it will seem too hard. Your tents will get stolen, your trucks will break down, you may be shot at, jailed or stoned, people will betray you, let you down. You'll have those days when you just don't want to do it anymore because you're feeling like *you* have to do it when in fact you can't do it. And that's the reality—we can't, but He can, so we will. **You can't accomplish what God wants you to accomplish or live like Jesus on the earth, but God living in you can do all things**. Christ in us is the hope of glory. You can give your life away with great joy and peace because He is in charge. Stress will fall away when you stop trying to figure it all out and simply let Him lead you. Lay your life down into His and He will make a way. His power is made perfect in our weakness.

REFLECTION QUESTIONS

1. Today, make the commitment to believe that God works out absolutely everything in conformity with the purpose of His will; then, as you encounter obstacles and difficulties, make a note of each one and then come back and note how God worked things out when you surrendered completely to Him.

_____
_____
_____
_____
_____
_____
_____
_____
_____

2. If you are someone who has trouble letting go and letting God, what are some of the obstacles and how can you get past them?

_____
_____
_____
_____
_____
_____
_____
_____
_____
_____

3. Be the "living word" to someone today and then note how they were impacted.

_____
_____
_____
_____
_____
_____
_____
_____

THE DNA OF FATHER GOD

"And surely I am with you always, to the very end of the age."
—Matthew 28:20

So many today struggle with an orphan spirit, unable to comprehend the Father's love for them. They go through life not having a secure, safe place where they feel affirmed and protected, unable to find identity and a place of belonging in God's love. When I was a little girl my dad would come home—he ran a very large company and always wore a suit—and the first thing he would do was take off his suit and put on his pink pants and play with us. The pink pants used to be red, but he loved them so much and wore them so much that they became pink from too many washings. As soon as he came through the door we would say, "Put on the pink pants, put on the pink pants," because we knew pink pants meant play time. He would capture my sister or me, and we'd wiggle, wiggle and he'd say, "You can't get out. You can't get out," and then suddenly he'd let us out, but he wouldn't let us know he let us out. It was wonderful! We'd feel so powerful! Dad would say, "Wow, you're so strong. You're amazing. You got out," but it was just that he let us out; he let us feel strong. Your heavenly Father is going to let you wiggle sometimes, try to find a solution, but He's always there as your Daddy to make you feel strong because He's in you just like the DNA of your earthly father is in you. God made us alive through Christ. We're no longer orphans. We're no longer pushed away. We are literally God's children.

Another fun game my dad and I would play was "walking on his feet." I would put my feet on top of his feet and hold his hands and he would say, "We're going places," and together we would "go" all over the world on great adventures. You see, God knew before I was even born that He and I would be going places together, all over the world. But I can't go anywhere on my own. **It's only when I stand on God's feet and hold His hands that I can go anywhere and do anything**. That's how it is with me and God, and it's the same for you. He lives in you. You're not alone. You are not an orphan. You have a safe and secure place in God's heart where you will find affirmation, protection, and true identity. Everywhere you go, you carry Christ with you. All you have to do it take your Father's hands and "step" on His feet and He will carry you anywhere. Together with Him, all things are possible.

REFLECTION QUESTIONS

1. What are some of the ways you see your heavenly Father's DNA in yourself?

2. Have you ever felt like God was pushing you away? If so, was it really God doing the pushing?

3. How do you see your place in God's heart?

STEP INTO YOUR DESTINY

"For we are his workmanship, created in Christ Jesus for good works,
which God prepared beforehand so that we would walk in them."
—Ephesians 2:10 NASB

I became a born-again Christian at the age of sixteen while serving as an American Field Service student on an Indian reservation in Mississippi. When I returned home to Laguna Beach my parents and teachers didn't know what to do with me. Suddenly I didn't fit. I was a Pentecostal Holiness teenager in a town that had no formal denominational churches. My parents tried to send me to a psychiatrist to try and de-program me but I refused to go. At the time I was enrolled in a special program at Laguna Beach High School. It was a special school for creative people. We sat around on pillows and drank herbal tea. People would come to school high on drugs, which was okay, but Pentecostal Holiness was definitely not okay. To make matters worse, I was severely dyslexic. My teacher at the time didn't like me and was actually quite mean to me. She would mock my efforts to spell (dyslexics have trouble spelling) and was constantly telling me that I would never go to university. She told me to forget about going to college; the only thing I was fit for was vocational school. The whole situation was a recipe for an orphan spirit, but thankfully my parents were very loving and affirming (of everything but my Christian faith) and so I was able to manage. Then one day, about two or three months after my born-again experience, I was powerfully healed of the dyslexia. Suddenly I was able to read perfectly and I became a speed reader.

During my born-again experience, God spoke to me telling me I was to be a minister and a missionary who would go to Africa, Asia, and England. I couldn't quite wrap my mind around that word, and with no one to counsel me in the things of God, I headed in another direction. With the words of my teacher ("Go to vocational school") ringing in my ears, and a word from a well meaning minister that I should be a nurse, I headed to nursing school via a vocational program. I thought I was doing the right thing. I went through nursing school and graduated but had absolutely no aptitude for nursing. It was pitiful, really. Nowadays I don't even like to tell people I'm a nurse because it isn't what God intended for me. Imagine if I had tried to go to Africa as a nurse! I would have missed my destiny entirely. I tried to squish myself into a box that wasn't right for me. But thanks be to God that He showed me my true destiny. I grew in my relationship with Him until I got to the point where I believed God instead of the people around me. God had a specific destiny for me and He has one for you. The Spirit of Adoption is on you. Receive it! Become who God intends you to be. You are His workmanship, created in Jesus for good works, which God prepared beforehand so that you would walk in them. **Start walking down God's path for you today**. The world is waiting for you!

REFLECTION QUESTIONS

1. Have you ever found yourself heading in the wrong direction, and if so what sent you down that path?

2. Are you listening to the people around you when it comes to your destiny in God, or are you listening to God? What is God saying to you?

3. What is the Spirit of Adoption?

YOU ARE GOD'S POSSESSION

"And you also were included in Christ when you heard the word of truth, the gospel of your salvation. Having believed, you were marked in Him with a seal, the promised Holy Spirit, who is a deposit guaranteeing our inheritance until the redemption of those who are God's possession—to the praise of His glory."
—EPHESIANS 1:13-14

Are all paintings beautiful? The sensible answer seems to be that not all of them are, only some of them. But perhaps all paintings *are* beautiful. Think about it. Every person is beautiful when you look at yourself as the canvas and God as the artist. It is then you understand that whatever He paints with your life becomes something lovely. I pray every day that God will pick me up like a paintbrush and paint a picture for the world that reflects His glory. Sometimes we take the brush and start splattering colors all over the canvas of our life until we look like a mess, and all the while God is standing by, waiting for us to give the brush back to Him so that He can make us more beautiful than before. He's the Master Artist. He has all the colors in the universe and all the talent in the universe. He makes *all* things beautiful.

It's so glorious to give yourself fully to God who is the One, to find out who you are, to allow God to paint your canvas. God says we are included in Christ (verse 13 of Ephesians 2), and having believed we are marked, chosen, sealed with the promised Holy Spirit who is the deposit guaranteeing our inheritance until the redemption of those who are God's possession to the praise of His glory! Wow! God's possession! We belong to God. But what do *you* think about God? It's important what you think about God and who you think He is—what you think He's like. It's important that you get a greater revelation of who God is because if you are His possession then you should know intimately the One who possesses you. You're His possession to the praise of His glory! That means you're called to carry the glory of God! How marvelous! How exciting! Who doesn't want to do that?

Become part of the family of God. Dwell together in His presence. Soak, pray, worship together. Enjoy Him together. Let possession by the Holy Spirit become your lifestyle. Press in for wisdom and revelation to know Him better. Learn what it means to abandon yourself into His arms, like a child, totally in love. **Dig deep with the Spirit for revelation to know who He is so that following Him becomes your greatest joy**. Hear His voice, feel His embrace. Become a lover of His presence.

REFLECTION QUESTIONS

1. Do you have a hard time thinking of yourself as a beautiful painting from the hand of God? If so, what is causing your difficulty?

_____
_____
_____
_____
_____
_____
_____
_____

2. What do you think about God? Who is He? What is He like?

_____
_____
_____
_____
_____
_____
_____
_____
_____
_____
_____
_____
_____
_____

3. What does God's embrace feel like to you?

_____
_____
_____
_____
_____
_____
_____
_____
_____
_____
_____
_____
_____

OVERSHADOWED BY HIS PRESENCE

Heidi Baker

"But even as He [Jesus] spoke, a bright cloud overshadowed them, and a voice from the cloud said, 'This is My dearly loved Son, who brings Me great joy. Listen to Him.'"
—MATTHEW 17:5 NLT

SESSION SUMMARY

God is inviting you into that place of holy encounter with Him. He wants to position you for His purposes, but first you must get into position. You must lay your life down, allowing yourself to be totally undone by God's magnificent presence until your every breath is given over to Him. **If you let Him, God will put such a hunger inside of you that you will be drawn to a place of holy encounter with Him where He will overshadow every aspect of who you are.** In this place of encounter He will put seeds in your heart and then so fill you with His Spirit that you will be able to sustain those seeds until His purposes are accomplished. Jesus is the Lord of the harvest, and He is inviting you into His glorious harvest fields!

God wants to put His favor on you so that you can participate with Him in His divine plan. You can't earn His favor or make it happen. Sometimes His favor doesn't look like what we expected or come when we expected. Often, those around you will not rejoice with you when God's favor comes upon you, but you must hold fast to what He puts in you, trusting in Him. No matter what you do, wherever you end up going for God, always remember that your destiny is to be fully possessed by God's holy presence. You are God's temple, His resting place, a reflection of His beauty.

Satan seeks to convince you of his lies instead of God's truth—to make you think you aren't really called by God, that all of this is just your imagination. And if he can't talk you out of your calling, he will try to convince you that it's not worth the price you will have to pay. In these moments you must know what it means to carry the promise that God has put inside of you. You must know that God's promise is precious. You must learn to nourish His promise, to hold fast in the face of opposition. No matter how impossible your promise may seem at times, if God put it in your heart, He will give you the ability to accomplish that to which He has called you. Every minute of every day is full of opportunities to live for God's glory. The choice is yours—choose to live each day for God no matter the circumstances because Jesus is altogether lovely, altogether worthy.

MAIN CONCEPTS FROM SESSION SEVEN

"But even as He [Jesus] spoke, a bright cloud overshadowed them, and a voice from the cloud said, 'This is My dearly loved Son, who brings Me great joy. Listen to Him.'"
—MATTHEW 17:5 NLT

OVERSHADOWED BY HIS PRESENCE

Heidi Baker

Holy Encounters: *"The Holy Spirit will come upon you, and the power of the Most High will overshadow you."* —Luke 1:35

- When you are moving in your God-given identity, you are ideally positioned for holy encounters.

- Holy encounters begin with a yielded life and a spiritual hunger.

- Embrace God's holy encounters and yield to His favor and glory.

- Go to a place of intimacy with God where He will plant His seeds in your heart.

- Allow the Holy Spirit to sustain you from "germination" through to the harvest.

- Seek experiential knowledge of Jesus that transforms every aspect of your life.

Highly Favored: *"If God is for us, who can be against us? He who did not spare His own Son, but gave Him up for us all—how will He not also, along with Him, graciously give us all things?"* —Romans 8:31-32

- God's overshadowing is powerful and glorious.

- When God overshadows you, He wants you to participate with Him.

- God's favor can be scary and "outside the box."

- "Outside the box" favor can be unexpected and inconvenient.

- Friends and family may reject what God's favor is doing in your life.

Grace for the Journey: *"I am sure of this, that He who started a good work in you will carry it on to completion until the day of Christ Jesus."* —Philippians 1:6 HCSB

- God's way of preparing you for missions may involve a period of upheaval.

- God will give you His grace in the times of upheaval.

- Always follow *God's* lead into the mission field.

- Don't try to be like someone else you see in the mission field.

- Training for missions isn't about filling someone else's shoes.

- Training for missions is about discovering who God is calling you to be and where He is calling you to go.

Carry the Promise: *"He called you to this through our gospel, that you might share in the glory of our Lord Jesus Christ."* —2 Thessalonians 2:14

- God will put a promise on your life when you say "Yes."

- Don't be afraid to carry that promise through to completion.

- Be willing to pay the price.

- Treasure God's promise—hold on to it, nourish it.

- Allow His Holy Spirit to enable you to do the impossible.

Fall on Your Knees: *"The testimony of Jesus is the spirit of prophecy."* —Revelation 19:10

- Learn to hold fast to Him and not give up.

- The best way to do this is on our knees.

- God provides.

- Live for the glory of God.

Session Seven Devotions

HOLY ENCOUNTERS

*"The Holy Spirit will come upon you, and the power
of the Most High will overshadow you."*
—LUKE 1:35

By now you should have a firm grasp on the importance of identity and how foundational it is in the life of every believer. Identity means freedom and intimacy with God. When you're moving in your identity you are ideally positioned for holy encounters. Mary, the mother of Jesus, is an amazing example of what a holy encounter looks like. The Lord God of the universe came and overshadowed Mary, and she was undone—so undone that she simply laid her life down before God. She gave Him everything. Mary was in a season of her life where she was able to embrace the encounter with God and yield to His favor and glory.

In this passage from Luke 1:35, an angel of the Lord tells Mary that the Holy Spirit is about to "come upon you." In the Greek, to "come upon" means that something is about to arrive or occur. Elsewhere in the gospels Jesus talks about the Holy Spirit coming upon people in power. God wants to arrive in your life and come upon you in power—power that sets you free and empowers you for service. Likewise, when the word "overshadow" is used in Matthew 17:5 and Acts 5:15 the Greek means to envelop you in a brilliant haze and to invest you with supernatural influence. This is the stuff of holy encounters!

If you let Him, God will put such a hunger inside of you that you will be drawn to a place of holy encounter with Him where He will overshadow every aspect of who you are. Like Mary, He will take you to a place of intimacy and invite you to participate in His divine plan. In this place of holy encounter He will put seeds in your heart and then so fill you with His Spirit that you will be able to sustain those seeds through germination and into the fruit-bearing stage and beyond. He is the Lord of the harvest, and He is inviting you into His glorious harvest fields! On the road to Damascus, Paul started out self-centered and ended up Christ-centered. His old nature was overshadowed by God's divine nature. In Philippians 3:8, Paul said, *"I consider everything a loss compared to the surpassing greatness of knowing Christ Jesus my Lord, for whose sake I have lost all things."* Paul isn't talking about knowledge gained through knowing facts about Jesus. He is talking about the experiential knowledge that comes from an intimate relationship with the living God that transforms one's entire person.

God wants to position you for His purposes, but first you must get in position. You must lay your life down, allowing yourself to be totally undone by His magnificent presence until your every breath is given over to Him. God is inviting you into that place of holy encounter. How will you respond?

REFLECTION QUESTIONS

1. What will it take today for you to allow yourself to be so totally undone by His magnificent presence that your every breath will be given over to Him?

_____

_____

_____

_____

_____

_____

_____

_____

_____

2. If you were to receive a holy encounter of the magnitude of Mary or Paul's encounter, how do you think you would react?

_____

_____

_____

_____

_____

_____

3. How would you define God's divine nature?

_____

_____

_____

_____

_____

_____

_____

HIGHLY FAVORED

"If God is for us, who can be against us? He who did not spare His own Son, but gave Him up for us all—how will He not also, along with Him, graciously give us all things?"
—Romans 8:31-32

Sometimes God's favor is bizarrely scary and amazingly beautiful all at the same time. Think of Mary, the mother of Jesus. Imagine her living in the 21st century. She's a fourteen-year-old girl living in a small town, and suddenly one day, out of nowhere, an angel appears to her and says, "Hi Mary. You're highly favored by God, and you're pregnant, by God." In one moment with God, Mary became a fourteen-year-old unmarried pregnant girl. To our natural minds that doesn't seem like favor. Notice that Scripture doesn't say that Mary sought God's favor. Perhaps she did, but from what we are told that wasn't the case. The point I want to make is that we don't earn God's favor and we can't make it happen, but, like Mary, when it comes upon us we need to learn how to steward it. Mary made the choice to participate with God. God wants to participate with you. The question is, do you want to participate with God? What if it's hard? What if participating with God isn't what you expected? What if it's inconvenient? What if your parents don't like it? What if your family and friends don't understand? Who will you respond to, the world or Jesus?

When I encountered God at the age of sixteen, it was very inconvenient for some people. My family totally rejected what had happened to me. They did everything they could to de-program Jesus out of me. They were hugely disappointed and quite upset with my God encounter. They absolutely did not want me "participating" with God or anything to do with God. I, on the other hand, was so overwhelmed and overshadowed by the presence of God that I was forever changed and nothing could change me back. I had encountered the living God, and like Paul on the road to Damascus and like Mary, I left behind the old and embraced the new because there is nothing else you can do when God becomes overwhelmingly real to you. My parents had plans for me that didn't include God, and they had invested heavily in those plans. But it was no use because I had heard the voice of my heavenly Father, felt His embrace, seen His heart.

When the favor of God comes upon you, not everybody is going to rejoice with you. Perhaps you have been fasting and praying for God's favor to fall on you, and suddenly you find yourself in this place where God shows up and covers your life with His glory and speaks something to you that you could not produce on your own. He speaks favor over you and destiny over you, and you know it is from Him, but it's not something you made happen. Now what do you do? How do you receive this favor and steward it well? I believe God wants to overshadow each and every one of us. He wants to put His favor on us so that we can participate with Him. **When we receive His favor and embrace it and run with it, He will come alongside us and continue to pour out His favor by His Spirit to help us carry that which He has put in us**. This overshadowing is holy; it's powerful. It's glorious. May a great hunger rise up in you now for more of God's overshadowing holy encounters! It has been one of my greatest privileges in life to lead both my father and mother to the Lord. My father was ordained as a minister at the age of 72. My mother came and served in Mozambique with us after my father went home to heaven. They saw the favor of God on our lives in Mozambique and they believed in beautiful Jesus!

REFLECTION QUESTIONS

1. If you have tried to earn God's favor or "make it happen," how did that turn out?

2. How do you respond when others are negative about God's call on your life?

3. God's ways sometimes seem so different, so odd, so scary. Imagine Mary's emotions when the reality of what God was doing became real in her life. What do you think it was that allowed her to embrace this unbelievably scary and yet amazingly beautiful thing God did?

GRACE FOR THE JOURNEY

"I am sure of this, that He who started a good work in you will carry it on to completion until the day of Christ Jesus."
—Philippians 1:6 HCSB

Some of you are going to discover while you're in the mission field in a third-world country that this is not what you're called to do, and that's okay. God never puts us in a box. You're going to be in your third day in the bush sitting in the dark, learning a language, and you're going to know that you know that you know that you're not called to cross-cultural ministry. You're going to get so excited at the revelation that this is not what you're called to do that you're going to start rejoicing! It's true. Training for missions isn't about filling someone else's shoes. It's about discovering who God is calling you to be and where He is calling you to go. You may think you're called to be a missionary in New York City, but when you start ministering there you realize that it's not the place God has for you. Don't put yourself in a box because someone else says that's where you should be or because you're trying to be like someone you admire in missions. Follow God's lead.

All that being said, there is often a time during training when you find yourself in an uncomfortable, in-between process. This is God getting you ready for what is to come. My parents had great ambitions for me to become a professional ballet dancer and invested heavily in those ambitions. They paid for years of dance lessons and I showed great promise. In fact, I loved ballet. I shared their ambitions until God got hold of me. And even then it was so very hard to lay my love of dance down for Him, but I did. There was a time when I took my toe shoes and literally laid them down before God. I gave it all to Him even though my heart was breaking over what seemed like a great loss. I cried like a baby when I laid down my ambitions. It was then that I began to learn that there is a process we go through with God, and that what He calls you to He will give you the grace for. He will give you tenacity and joy and grace for the journey. He will take you from the struggle to the joy.

Whatever you do, wherever you end up going for God, always remember that first and foremost your destiny is to be fully possessed by God's holy presence. Whether you come before kings or walk with paupers, teach at a university or live in a slum, you are a carrier of God's glory. You are His temple, His resting place, a reflection of His beauty.

REFLECTION QUESTIONS

1. If you have experienced that uncomfortable, in-between process that was described, how has it impacted you?

---

2. Reflect on whether or not you could be satisfied to be fully possessed by God's holy presence even if He never sent you into the mission field. What would that look like for you?

3. What does God's grace for your journey look like?

CARRY THE PROMISE

"He called you to this through our gospel, that you might
share in the glory of our Lord Jesus Christ."
—2 Thessalonians 2:14

I was invited to preach at a combined meeting of MIT and Harvard students and faculty. Both schools are very elite institutions. MIT is one of the most significant scientific institutions in the world. There were philosophers and theologians and scientists there, and lots of students. The place was full, jammed packed. The title of the conference was "Could Love Change the World?" The Lord told me not to do anything different for these people than I normally do, just to do what I do when I am in His presence—to call them to a radical place of missions. So I preached the Gospel and then I heard the Lord say that He was going to give someone a cure for AIDS and a cure for malaria, and that there would be radical, glorious scientific experimental things that God would put His holy glory on that would benefit many. I spoke these things out and then I gave an altar call. I called those brilliant minds into missions, into a life of radical love. I called them to lay down their life for Jesus' sake and to give it all to Him and wait to see what He would do. And then the most glorious encounter happened. The students rushed to the front and fell screaming and shaking on the altar. God had the meeting. It was sovereign, holy, totally in the hands of the Holy Spirit.

There was one very petite Asian girl shaking and screaming at the top of her lungs in the corner. I could see the power and the fire of God on her. I made my way to her, knelt beside her and said, "Sweetheart, what is going on?" "It's me. It's me," she screamed. "I'm just finishing my Ph.D. and I've been working all this time on a cure for AIDS and right now God is downloading on me from heaven. I'm hearing Him!" What a glorious, holy time it was to see God crashing in on these brilliant minds! I believe that when we see the cure for AIDS this brilliant Asian girl will be at the forefront, and I believe she is going to give all the glory to God!

Satan wants to tell God's people not to pay the price. He wants to convince you that you weren't really called to the third world, or to the inner city, or to the university, or to wherever it is that God has called you. He wants to convince you that what you thought was God calling you was really just your imagination. But when you have a promise from the Most High God, when God puts something inside of you, that something is precious. Don't treat God's precious gift as something insignificant. Hold on to God's promises and don't let go. Nourish what He puts inside of you. Carry the promise. **God will put the impossible in your heart and your mind and then He will give you the ability to accomplish His purposes.** The cure for AIDS won't come from a person. It will come from heaven itself, when the King of Glory crashes into the brilliant mind of the one who says, "Yes, Lord!" Will you pay the price, carry the promise, say "Yes" today?

REFLECTION QUESTIONS

1. How does the idea of being a "missionary" who finds a cure for something like AIDS while a student at a prestigious university fit with your concept of missions?

2. Do you think it is necessary to have a precious deposit from God in your heart that is so significant that you will do whatever it takes to nourish it even in the face of impossible odds, or can anyone who simply loves the Lord do missions? Explain your answer.

FALL ON YOUR KNEES

"The testimony of Jesus is the spirit of prophecy."
—Revelation 19:10

At Iris Global we are constantly challenged in every way. People who are new to the ministry often get nervous when they see the enormous challenges we face, and so we have to reassure them that God has not changed. He isn't shaking in His boots because of the challenges. If you are going to align yourself with the will of God, you can't spend time contemplating the worst. Instead, you must learn to hold fast to Him and not give up. At Iris we find the best way to do this is on our knees. When the challenges come, we fall on our knees and start lifting up songs of worship. **We get in the dirt and we worship God until His presence comes and He brings us peace, and in the midst of His peace we remember His provision**.

We were in the middle of a staff meeting one day, discussing some of our financial challenges, and I noticed that some of our new people were looking very anxious, so I asked one of our Mozambican spiritual sons to share some of the stories of God's faithfulness. As he spoke he began to weep at the goodness of God. He told of the times when machine guns were held at my head and knives at my throat, of the many times we had thousands to feed and no food or money, of the time the government took our buildings and were living in tents in the sand with worms biting us, and the time a land mine blew up when one of the children ran under the power lines, and yet in all of this God provided. We are still here. We feed many thousands a day, often because God multiplies food. It happens all the time. We no longer live in a tent. We have a base with housing because God provides. Now we only live in tents a few days a week on outreach. Because God provides we have a network of thousands of churches and schools and outreach programs. These testimonies of Jesus speak prophetically into our present circumstances and into our future and they are available to encourage you wherever God calls you to be. The Spirit of our risen King Jesus is the empowering source of our testimony.

Every moment of the day is filled with opportunities for us to live for the glory of God. We must choose each day to live for Him, no matter the circumstances, because Jesus is altogether lovely, altogether worthy. The challenges of the mission field are many. Here in Mozambique we are always challenged, but we are always blessed too. We fight the enemy without and the enemy within on our knees or on our faces, hands and voices lifted in praise to the One who is worthy of it all.

REFLECTION QUESTIONS

1. If you are faced with overwhelming challenges, how are you inclined to respond?

_____

_____

_____

2. What does it mean to fight the enemy without and within?

3. Share a testimony of Jesus from your life that speaks prophetically into your present circumstances.

Session Eight

JOY

Rolland Baker

"To grant those who mourn in Zion, giving them a garland instead of ashes, the oil of gladness instead of mourning, the mantle of praise instead of a spirit of fainting. So they will be called oaks of righteousness, the planting of the Lord, that He may be glorified."
—Isaiah 61:3 NASB

SESSION SUMMARY

Joy is not optional for the Christian life. When we don't enjoy God, He doesn't feel loved or truly honored, but when we are joyful God is pleased. Our joy reflects our confidence in Him. We need to live daily crushed by our own weakness but amazed by God, overwhelmed and thrilled with Him, living with a childlike faith and joy that is beyond understanding. We need to allow this inexpressible joy, this river of living water to flow freely in us and through us. When joyful rivers of living water flow out of us in the power of the Holy Spirit, His manifest presence will fill us with strength and motivation to do His will. He is our portion and our cup. His joy is our strength and our greatest weapon against the enemy. When we rejoice in the Lord in spite of Satan's attacks, we disarm the devil. As we pursue Him, the impossible is transformed into joyful and exciting adventure. This dichotomy in the Christian life—that it is both hard and easy—brings supernatural balance to everything we do. God shows Himself strong when we are weak.

God's variety in relating to human beings is astonishing. Each one of us must find Him, know Him, and become one in spirit with Him according to our unique personalities. No amount of training and no program can make that happen without God. Apart from His grace and self-revelation, we are nothing. Discipleship is a living process, dancing, glowing and sparking with life, colors and flavors. We are constantly seeing and comprehending with new eyes, forgetting what lies behind and pressing forward to what lies ahead. It is in the midst of this process that we find our joy.

MAIN CONCEPTS FROM SESSION EIGHT

"Be joyful in hope, patient in affliction, faithful in prayer."
—Romans 12:12

JOY

Rolland Baker

Joy Is Imperative: *"For we are the aroma of Christ to God among those who are being saved and among those who are perishing, to one a fragrance from death to death, to the other a fragrance from life to life. Who is sufficient for these things? For we are not, like so many, peddlers of God's word, but as men of sincerity, as commissioned by God, in the sight of God we speak in Christ."* —2 Corinthians 2:15–17 ESV

- Joy is not optional for the Christian life. It is imperative.

- Nothing that we want in the Christian life has meaning without joy.

- God doesn't feel loved if we don't enjoy Him.

- Our confidence in Him is reflected in our joy.

- All true theology leads to joy.

- Joy is the energy of the Holy Spirit.

- Joy was the reward the Father gave Jesus.

Our Greatest Weapon: *"The Lord is my strength and my shield; my heart trusts in Him, and I am helped."* —Psalm 28:7

- Actively engaging in God's joy—singing, praising God, praying fervently—pushes back Satan's attacks.

- The joy of the Lord always brings hope.

- Joy in the midst of great hardship leads to great freedom.

- The goodness and joy of the Gospel happens when we are free from sin.

- The joy of the Lord is explosive, bringing power, energy, and passion for the lost.

Perspectives: *"We are hard pressed on every side, but not crushed; perplexed, but not in despair; persecuted, but not abandoned; struck down, but not destroyed. We always carry around in our body the death of Jesus,* *so that the life of Jesus may also be revealed in our body. For we who are alive are always being given over to death for Jesus' sake, so that His life may be revealed in our mortal body. So then, death is at work in us, but life is at work in you."* —2 Corinthians 4:8–12

- The Christian life is both hard and easy.

- The difficult aspects of Christian life make us stronger spiritually.

- Spiritual strength is a necessity for the mission field.

- We are called to do the impossible in order to prove the power and quality of our faith.

- Our faith will be tested to the limit to show what kind of relationship we have with God.

Jars of Clay: *"But He said to me, 'My grace is sufficient for you, for My power is made perfect in weakness.' Therefore I will boast all the more gladly about my weaknesses, so that Christ's power may rest on me."* —2 Corinthians 12:9

- In the midst of our worst suffering we can find our greatest joy.

- This is a supernatural joy that comes as we draw close to Jesus.

- Joy motivated Jesus on the cross (see Heb. 12:2).

- Our weakness is our opportunity to display His strength.

- We must become clay on His potter's wheel in order to be formed into His likeness, becoming servants who joyfully display His love and goodness in all circumstances.

The Surpassing Glory of God: *"I delight greatly in the Lord; my soul rejoices in my God. For He has clothed me with garments of salvation and arrayed me in a robe of righteousness, as a bridegroom adorns his head like a priest, and as a bride adorns herself with her jewels."* —Isaiah 61:10

- The amazing things God is doing through Iris are not because of anything we do.

- The circumstances are so overwhelmingly impossible that any and every success comes from God alone, from His surpassing glory.

- If we consider ourselves to be amazing people because of what God has done, others will look to us instead of to God.

Session Eight Devotions

JOY IS IMPERATIVE

"For we are the aroma of Christ to God among those who are being saved
and among those who are perishing, to one a fragrance from death to death,
to the other a fragrance from life to life. Who is sufficient for these things?
For we are not, like so many, peddlers of God's word, but as men of sincerity,
as commissioned by God, in the sight of God we speak in Christ."
—2 CORINTHIANS 2:15–17 ESV

God doesn't feel loved if we don't enjoy Him—constantly, in all things, to overflowing. Our confidence in Him is reflected in our joy. Life without joy is absolutely pointless. What is the point of giving everything to God—of laying your life down, suffering, serving Him, doing everything He says—if we don't enjoy God? Hebrews 1:9 says, *"You have loved righteousness and hated wickedness; therefore God, your God, has set you above your companions by anointing you with the oil of joy."*

What would we possibly trade joy for? People say, "I just want Jesus." Really, without joy? Or, "Oh, I just want love." Really, without joy? "I just want to go to heaven." Really, without joy? "I want to see lots of people saved." Really, without joy? "I want my shadow to heal people." Really, without joy? Joy was the motivation that led Jesus through the cross. It was also His reward.

I take joy extremely seriously because no matter how you slice it, no matter what you do with theology or the truth, eventually you're going to end up with joy. Joy is actually *life*. Without it we are spiritually dead. **The joy of the Lord is the energy of the Holy Spirit.** This unfettered, uncontrolled, outlandish, over-the-top volcanic joy is also the most controversial thing in the Church. It can be the most suspicious, most aggravating, most irritating aspect of life in the Spirit, and the first thing the devil wants to steal from you. Many consider it unnecessary, and yet for us it is not optional! Joy is the outcome of the Christian life! Without it we die!

REFLECTION QUESTIONS

1. How can a person take joy extremely seriously?

_____

_____

_____

_____

_____
_____
_____
_____
_____
_____
_____
_____

2. What does Rolland mean when he says the joy of the Lord is the energy of the Holy Spirit?

_____
_____
_____
_____
_____
_____
_____
_____
_____
_____
_____
_____
_____

3. Why is joy one of the most controversial things in the Church?

_____
_____
_____
_____
_____
_____
_____
_____
_____
_____
_____

OUR GREATEST WEAPON

"The Lord is my strength and my shield; my heart trusts in Him, and I am helped."
—Psalm 28:7

In 1995 Heidi and I began working with a dilapidated children's institution in Mozambique. Chihango was a picture of hell on earth. In this government-sponsored institution, eighty children huddled, deprived of even the most basic necessities, starving, filthy, living like animals in buildings stripped bare by dangerous, violent bandits. The children and meager staff were without hope. We when first arrived we didn't have much to offer them materially, but we did bring them into contact with the Spirit of God, and slowly they responded. They learned to sing songs of praise and to laugh, and though they were malnourished, filled with parasites and disease, abandoned and forgotten, they received the story of Jesus and began to embrace His joy.

The children of Chihango learned to pray with all their hearts, exalting Jesus and resisting the devil, singing throughout the day with life and hope. They became sponges soaking up the Holy Spirit, fully expecting God to provide for them and their future. They knew they were made for God, made for the glory of His presence, made to encounter Him. They understood the joy of the Lord, and it became their greatest weapon against the enemy. Even in the midst of great hardship, they were free.

The Church will try and tell you that the Christian life is all about self-sacrifice and self-denial. It's true. Jesus did say, "Deny yourself, take up your cross, and follow Me" (see Matt. 16:24), but He wasn't trying to kill our joy. He was instructing us to get rid of the sins in our lives that rob us of our freedom and joy. **The goodness of God brings freedom from sin, and that is the open door to joy.**

REFLECTION QUESTIONS

1. How much joy do you find in your relationship with God?

----

2. How would you explain joy as a weapon?

3. How do you fail to appreciate the joy of the Lord?

PERSPECTIVES

"We are hard pressed on every side, but not crushed; perplexed, but not in despair; persecuted, but not abandoned; struck down, but not destroyed. We always carry around in our body the death of Jesus, so that the life of Jesus may also be revealed in our body. For we who are alive are always being given over to death for Jesus' sake, so that His life may be revealed in our mortal body. So then, death is at work in us, but life is at work in you."
—2 Corinthians 4:8–12

Years ago, Pastor Yonggi Cho preached at a huge revival in Korea. Part of his message was that every year he expected to have the greatest crisis of his life. I had trouble with that part of the message because at that point in my life I had been listening to Christian teaching that said we're not supposed to suffer any kind of crisis, and that it's not God's will for us to suffer. Eventually I realized the foolishness of this kind of thinking. If we're to be greatly honored, glorified and rewarded in heaven, how can we expect that without having our faith tested and proven to be genuine? And that may involve temporary suffering—under God's control. Do we think God's going to reward us for sitting around on easy street every day of our lives? The great apostle Paul despaired even of life at times.. The apostle Peter said, *"Do not be surprised at the painful trial you are suffering"* (1 Pet. 4:12), *"because you know that your brothers throughout the world are undergoing the same kind of sufferings"* (1 Pet. 5:9). We should not to be surprised by difficulties and challenges, but many of us are.

Many people ask me if the Christian life is hard or easy. My response is always that is depends on your perspective. The Christian life is both extremely easy and extremely hard. If it were always easy we wouldn't grow, get more faith and get more strength. We would suffer from a lack of spiritual fitness. You don't stay physically fit by sitting around. You actually have to exercise. It's the same with spiritual fitness.

The Christian life can be extremely challenging. We are called to do the impossible, to overcome, to be more than conquerors. Yet these challenges are opportunities to prove the power and the quality of our faith, the depth of our love for God, and our trust in Him. You are made for the glory of His presence, especially in the midst of trials and troubles. Encounter Him! Cry out for more fire! More signs and wonders! More gifts of the Spirit! More intimacy! More love and joy! More fruit! Never settle for an average, mundane, "normal Christian life." Learn to totally enjoy every aspect of our amazing God.

REFLECTION QUESTIONS

1. How do you view the aspect of suffering in the Christian life?

_____

_____

_____

_____

2. What do you think about Rolland's statement that our reward in heaven comes about in part through our suffering here on earth?

3. How spiritually fit are you?

JARS OF CLAY

"But He said to me, 'My grace is sufficient for you, for My power is made perfect in weakness.' Therefore I will boast all the more gladly about my weaknesses, so that Christ's power may rest on me."
—2 Corinthians 12:9

In our outreaches, thousands find joy as they listen to the Gospel. Most are desperate, weak, and sick, without possessions, yet they are thrilled to sit and learn about our Lord Jesus. They worship and pray and weep in repentance; they sing and dance rejoicing in the joy of the risen Savior. They need the Lord and all that is in His heart, and they find it in Jesus. Joy becomes an incredible, motivating force in their lives, just as it was for Jesus on the cross. Hebrews 12:2 says, *"Jesus…for the joy set before Him endured the cross, scorning its shame, and sat down at the right hand of the throne of God."*

If Jesus needed the power of that kind of joy, so do we. The prospect of such great joy got Him through the cross. This same kind of joy will get us through our fiery trials. We have seen it happen over and over again in Mozambique. In the midst of our worst suffering we find our greatest joy. It is a supernatural joy that comes as we draw close to Jesus. Our weakness is made perfect in Him. We are His jars of clay, always willing to be put on the "potter's wheel." As ministers of the Gospel, we are fragile, weak vessels. When others see our weaknesses, it becomes obvious that power belongs to God and not to us.

As apostles and ministers of the Gospel, death is at work in us, from one perspective. Paul comments that apostles are the outcasts of the world, the ones displayed last of all. That is our calling—to be the least, the lowest, to be the servant of all, the slave of all, because that's where God is with us and we find our joy.

REFLECTION QUESTIONS

1. How willing are you for others to see your weaknesses?

_____

_____

_____

_____

_____

_____

_____

2. What do you make of Rolland's statement that without joy it is nearly impossible to make it on the mission field?

3. What does it mean to you to "need the Lord and all that is in His heart"?

THE SURPASSING GLORY OF GOD

"I delight greatly in the Lord; my soul rejoices in my God. For He has clothed me with garments of salvation and arrayed me in a robe of righteousness, as a bridegroom adorns his head like a priest, and as a bride adorns herself with her jewels."
—Isaiah 61:10

They come without food, without shoes, with swollen, infected eyes and feet, and terrible scabs and sores. We feed them, give them straw mats to sleep on, and tell them of the love of Jesus. They flood into the meetings, kneeling in the dust and hot sun throughout the day and into the dark night. As the conviction and joy of the Lord settles on them, they begin to throw themselves before God. A mighty cry of prayer goes up to heaven as young and old alike weep rivers of tears, hands stretched out to God. A mighty outpouring of the Holy Spirit brings the richest love in the universe crashing down like a mighty river on hungry hearts.

The joy of the Lord is explosive! It brings power, energy and a passion for the lost. Many are the days when we have arrived back home in Pemba dirty, hot, perspiring, with clothes soggy and feet caked with dust and mud. Our creaking old Land Rover is loaded down, the bench seats in the back jammed with Mozambican ministry buddies and short-term visitors. We are one happy family after pouring out all we could on yet another village in the bush. With piles of equipment and supplies stuffed between us, we are stiff and hot, but we have been talking nonstop on the long ride back home about the sheer joy of serving the King among some of the poorest people on earth. We are awed and thrilled that God would tangibly enter our meetings, touch our bodies, and fill us to overflowing with love and joy—inexpressible and full of glory. We know we are made for joy, made for God.

Everything good and fruitful about Iris results quite apart from anything we have done. Those who have long been with us are convinced of that! Given that we are just weak vessels struggling in the midst of the impossible in Mozambique, Iris shouldn't exist, but it does. It's obvious that the transcendent power belongs to God and not to us (see 2 Cor. 4:7). **He is able to glorify Himself in ways that keep attention on Him.** We have been humbled and broken to the utmost, with absolutely nothing to recommend us in view of the surpassing glory of God. This is what the world needs to understand.

REFLECTION QUESTIONS

1. How does a person apprehend the glory of God?

_____

_____

_____

_____

_____

_____

_____

_____

_____

2. What does Rolland mean when he says the joy of the Lord is explosive?

_____

_____

_____

_____

_____

_____

_____

_____

_____

_____

3. Why do you think Iris is still going after all these years? Is it because of the material support they have received?

_____

_____

_____

_____

_____

_____

_____

_____

_____

_____

Session Nine

A YIELDED LIFE AND UNDIVIDED HEART

Rolland Baker

"The eyes of the Lord range throughout the earth to strengthen those whose hearts are fully committed to Him."
—2 Chronicles 16:9

SESSION SUMMARY

God is looking for radical lovers who are not afraid to surrender all, willingly accepting His sovereignty. He wants yielded lives and undivided hearts. He is seeking those who are willing to become nothing so that He can become everything in them. The more we acknowledge our weakness and helplessness, the more the power of God rests on us. Then His gifts impel us toward that glorious union where fruits of character are joined by gifts of power.

The Christian life is about discovering the infinite perfection of Jesus that surpasses anything this world has to offer, and then being drawn into an ultimate love affair withour perfect Lover. Satan will do all that he can to keep that from happening. His goal is to tear humanity away from God, but Jesus, our triumphant Lover, is able to capture us and keep us safe in His heart. When we join our ourselves to Him we begin laying up treasure in heaven, all those things that intensify our relationship with Him.

We must be led by the Spirit, even in our weakness, unwilling to settle for anything less than the pearl of great price, Jesus Himself. He is the point of life, the reason for our existence. He is divisive because He is God, and there is no other alternative, however much mankind may resist Him and His perfect holiness. In our sin we refuse the light, but Jesus by His Spirit is able to overcome.

MAIN CONCEPTS FROM SESSION NINE

"The eyes of the Lord range throughout the earth to strengthen
those whose hearts are fully committed to Him."
—2 Chronicles 16:9

A Yielded Life and Undivided Heart

Rolland Baker

God Is Not Seeker-Sensitive: *"The sacrifices of God are a broken spirit; a broken and contrite heart, O God, You will not despise."* —Psalm 51:17

- The Gospel is divisive; there is no other alternative, yet many resist in their sin.

- Jesus is the manifestation of the one true God, and we have no hope in anyone else.

- Jesus brings the kingdom of God, and repentance is the only way to face it.

- The poor in spirit can more easily see God, more willingly accept God's sovereignty, and are not afraid to surrender all because they know how much they need Him.

- The poor in spirit need Jesus, not just teachings, principles and abstract ideas.

The Nature of Free Will: *"Those who live according to the sinful nature have their minds set on what that nature desires; but those who live in accordance with the Spirit have their minds set on what the Spirit desires."* —Romans 8:5

- In the upside-down nature of the kingdom, sovereignty means freedom, the freedom to obey God voluntarily as the Holy Spirit changes our hearts..

- Everything in us that is not from the Holy Spirit will be destroyed.

- Our will can never improve on God's will, or make us happier than His.

- Real goodness comes from God and not from us.

Mature in Christ: *"That you may stand firm in all the will of God, mature and fully assured."* —Colossians 4:12

- Maturity is the loss of all confidence in ourselves, and total confidence in Jesus.

- We acknowledge our weaknesses that the power of God may rest on us.

- Union with God is a union of character and gifts of power.

- The only way forward in Jesus is to go lower still, and then go even lower.

Basic Christian Life: *"For I know the plans I have for you,' declares the Lord, 'plans to prosper you and not to harm you, plans to give you hope and a future.'"* —Jeremiah 29:11

- The Christian life in this world is preparation for the next, keeping an eternal perspective.

- The Christian life is the discovery that Jesus is so infinitely perfect that nothing in world that attracts you more than Him.

- Our hearts cannot be set on both this life *and* the next.

- Our main concern should be attaining to the resurrection from the dead in Christ.

- The Christian life is an ultimate love affair that the enemy strives to obstruct.

- The issue of heaven and hell is primary in life.

Union with Christ: *"I want to know Christ and the power of His resurrection and the fellowship of sharing in His sufferings, becoming like Him in His death, and so, somehow, to attain the resurrection from the dead."* —Philippians 3:10-11

- We aim to know the power of His resurrection, and to participate in His sufferings, becoming like Him in His death.

- Righteousness and union with Christ are inseparable.

- Treasure in heaven is laid up by acts of righteousness.

Session Nine Devotions

GOD IS NOT SEEKER-SENSITIVE

*"The sacrifices of God are a broken spirit; a broken and
contrite heart, O God, You will not despise."*
—Psalm 51:17

March 2000: Southern Mozambique is one huge flood plain draining the highlands of South Africa and Zimbabwe, and there is no escape for whole towns and villages, many still beyond the reach of rescue helicopters. Mothers struggling in neck-deep currents drown their own babies in their back slings. Stranded communities are reduced to eating the decayed flesh of dead cows, and children are even roasting rats. Upper-story roofs collapse under the weight of so many desperate survivors. The stench in the streets from sewage and animal carcasses is terrible. Severe malnutrition is setting in among young children. Clean water is nearly impossible to find. Malaria victims lie motionless in the dirt with high fevers. Twenty-six camps with almost no facilities or provisions are trying to care for 250,000 people.

Yet in the camps we find huge joy as thousands listen to the Gospel and devour tracts even before they eat the bread we bring. We need truckloads of tracts and Bibles to satisfy such hunger. Weak, sick, and without possessions, these flood victims are thrilled to sit and learn about our Lord Jesus. There is no need for seeker-sensitive church here. These people want the real thing. They need God and all that is in His heart. They aren't afraid to surrender all. They willingly accept the sovereignty of God, but we in the West struggle, not wanting to be controlled by anyone, especially God. We want religion that gives us a God who will respect our individuality. I hear people say they don't pray often because they don't want God invading their space!

The Church today is full of ministries that try to make Christianity less "toxic," to talk more about things that people will be interested in. They try to make church palatable and inviting. Jesus didn't come to have a dialogue with us about our interests. He came to tell us to repent, for the kingdom of God is at hand. His message was anything but seeker-sensitive. He didn't come to tell us that there are many ways to get to heaven. **He was very explicit that He is the way, the truth, and the life, the only way to the Father.** This is a hard message for us today. We want peace. We want to make people of other faiths feel good. We shy away from being divisive with the Gospel. Jesus is either extremely good news or really terrible news. There is no in between. His message is divisive. He wants it all—a yielded life and an undivided heart.

REFLECTION QUESTIONS

1. The poor of the world live in great poverty but find it easy to become rich in spirit. Why is poverty of spirit so prevalent among those who have much?

2. How does the idea of having a broken spirit and a contrite heart make you feel?

3. James 4:6 says, *"God opposes the proud but gives grace to the humble."* Why do the humble receive grace?

THE NATURE OF FREE WILL

"Those who live according to the sinful nature have their minds set on what that nature desires; but those who live in accordance with the Spirit have their minds set on what the Spirit desires."
—ROMANS 8:5

Can anyone choose to do that which is perfect? Can you just get up in the morning and choose absolute righteousness for the whole day? Can anybody choose to be holy and love their neighbor as themselves all day long? Can you just choose to be thrilled and happy all the time? We are constantly told that happiness is a choice, but try choosing it when you're deep in clinical depression and demons are all over you and you're dying and everything is going wrong. You can't choose to be thrilled. You can't choose to be perfect. You can't choose to be exactly like Jesus. **We are completely dependent on God to do anything that is truly good.** No one can decide to do something with an absolutely pure motive, with no selfishness and no personal agenda involved. That level of perfection is a gift from God.

Many of us get into that place in life where things are going well. We feel confident, well adjusted, reasonably sure about our future. We have goals, interesting things we want to do in life and we really don't feel the need to involve God. We feel like we've "got it covered." Sure, we'll call on God if we really get into a bind, but otherwise we don't want His interference. Our notion of the nature of free will translates into an equation where we are in control, not God. We just can't wrap our minds around the upside-down nature of the kingdom of God. We have read the Scriptures, but submission has such a negative connotation that we inwardly reject the Word in favor of our own word. We may be making our own choices, but we are bound by our sin nature. Without the Spirit of the Lord in us, controlling us, we're anything but free.

The apostle Peter had a hard time understanding the nature of free will during his time as a disciple of Jesus. He was constantly charging ahead on his own with a brash confidence. As the time of His death drew closer, *"Jesus began to explain to His disciples that He must go to Jerusalem and suffer many things at the hands of the elders, chief priests and teachers of the law, and that He must be killed and on the third day be raised to life. Peter took him aside and began to rebuke Him. 'Never, Lord!' he said. 'This shall never happen to You!'"* (Matt. 16:21-22). Jesus' response defines the true nature of free will: *"Get behind Me, Satan! You are a stumbling block to Me; you do not have in mind the things of God, but the things of men"* (Matt. 16:23).

Are you ready to get upside down with God—to choose to be nothing so that you can become everything He intends? To choose the things of God, not the things of man?

REFLECTION QUESTIONS

1. What changed the disciple Peter into the apostle Peter?

2. Why is it not possible for us to choose to be perfect?

3. How does God's definition of free will keep us in a place of balance?

MATURE IN CHRIST

"That you may stand firm in all the will of God, mature and fully assured."
—COLOSSIANS 4:12

Everything we know about "growing up" in the natural is in direct opposition to what it means to mature in the Christian life. To mature in Christ is to grow less confident in yourself—less confident in your message, your ministry work, your health, in everything—until finally, hopefully, you have lost all confidence in anything but Jesus. When you're young and healthy and ambitious and trained and talented and beautiful, you want lots of freedom from God. But over the course of time, God will use life experience to teach you about the nature of sin so that what seemed acceptable a year ago isn't acceptable any more. In Second Corinthians we see the apostle Paul going through this process of losing all confidence in himself. He begins comfortably enough in chapter 1, but by chapter 12 he is declaring, *"Therefore I will boast all the more gladly about my weaknesses, so that Christ's power may rest on me. That is why, for Christ's sake, I delight in weaknesses, in insults, in hardships, in persecutions, in difficulties. For when I am weak, then I am strong"* (2 Cor. 12:9-10).

So often in our years as missionaries of the Gospel, Heidi and I have fallen short of comprehending and apprehending God to the fullest extent possible. Jesus is constantly proving Himself better than we think. We are astounded by our own dullness and lack of faith. Daily we must repent of our past misjudgments. **Our own pride and self-confidence are the biggest obstacles to our ministry.** The more we acknowledge our weaknesses and helplessness, the more the power of God rests on us. He is able and willing to pour out His Spirit without measure. We love His gifts. They propel us toward that glorious union with God where fruits of character are joined by gifts of power so that our lives reflect His glory and presence. Every day we learn more of what it means to be a friend of God. We understand that the only way forward is low and slow. We grow up in Christ more every day, on our knees, on our faces, in the dirt, learning to love like He loves.

REFLECTION QUESTIONS

1. Spend time reading Second Corinthians in its entirety. What happened to Paul to cause him to understand the true nature of "growing up" in Christ?

_____
_____
_____
_____
_____
_____

2. How has God used life experiences to teach you about the nature of sin?

_____
_____
_____
_____
_____
_____
_____
_____
_____
_____
_____
_____

3. What things are unacceptable to you now that were acceptable a year ago?

_____
_____
_____
_____
_____
_____
_____
_____
_____
_____
_____

BASIC CHRISTIAN LIFE

"'For I know the plans I have for you,' declares the Lord, 'plans to prosper you and not to harm you, plans to give you hope and a future.'"
—JEREMIAH 29:11

The Christian life is not about this world or anything in this world. It's about the fact that you have discovered something so precious and beautiful, so wonderfully overwhelming and desirable, so infinitely perfect that there's nothing in this earth that attracts you more. You are absolutely without even the slightest hesitation, willing to count as rubbish and throw away anything and everything in this world because your heart is set on the next world. Every temptation the devil tries to come at you with, every offering, every promise, every enticement, every possibility of an outstanding life on earth, you consider nothing compared to what's to come. This is the essence of the Christian life, and it begins with the question, "What must I do to inherit eternal life?"

Most people don't want to think too much about eternal life. They take the attitude that they'll worry about it when it comes. "You can't know anyway, so why think about it?" is a common refrain. They go about life on earth unconcerned about their eternal destination. If they only knew what was around the corner. If they only knew what hell was like. Hell is vastly more horrifying than one could ever imagine, and heaven is vastly better than we can possibly imagine. It is that choice between heaven and hell that each one of us should be paying attention to—serious attention. Life is short and could end at any moment.

Your heart cannot be divided, set in more than one place at a time. You cannot have your heart set on this life and on the next. The Christian life is not about here and now and heaven eventually, with unlimited blessings while we are on earth. **The true nature of the Christian life is about an ultimate love affair and an enemy who wants to keep you from that love affair.** This is a terrible situation, and we didn't ask for it. The human predicament is a terrible thing. We actually have a real devil who has caused the world to fall. We're living in the middle of a huge spiritual war and the situation is extremely serious. Our main concern should not be about obtaining any sort of thing on this earth but making sure we end up with a future. It's our eternal future that's at stake. Each and every one of us should be asking, "What must I do to be saved? What must I do to inherit eternal life?" God has given us a hope and a future in Jesus Christ. We must do our utmost to receive what He has so lovingly given.

REFLECTION QUESTIONS

1. How do you answer the question, "What must I do to inherit eternal life?"

2. Describe heaven and hell as you understand them.

3. What is getting in the way of you setting your heart on heaven instead of this world?

UNION WITH CHRIST

*"I want to know Christ and the power of his resurrection and the
fellowship of sharing in His sufferings, becoming like Him in His death,
and so, somehow, to attain the resurrection from the dead."*
—PHILIPPIANS 3:10-11

A principle benefit of union with Christ is righteousness, the gift from God that lays up treasure in heaven. Like Paul, I want to know Jesus. This "knowing" is not just encountering Him or experiencing His power. It is not just manifestations or visions. You can have all these experiences and barely know Jesus, barely be connected to Him. Union with Christ is so much more than supernatural encounters. True union with Christ means that you know Him personally, know how He thinks, know the power of His resurrection, and desire to participate with Him in everything including suffering, even unto death. This depth of intimacy goes beyond gaining knowledge *about* Jesus. We can know a lot about a person just by reading about them or hearing about them even though we have never met them. That's not a relationship. Jesus wants you to draw close and open your heart so that He can cleanse you. He wants you to taste and see the righteousness of God that is imputed to all who believe in Jesus.

We are pilgrims and strangers on the earth, camping deep in enemy territory on our way to heaven. We are here to do the will of the Father. Because of Jesus, we cannot lose no matter how many times we turn the other cheek and walk the second mile. Our goal in all of life should be to be where Jesus is—to pay any price. As soon as we set our hearts on things here on earth, we are lost. But if your heart is set on Jesus Himself, then He's free to bless you. We need to *"be found in Him, not having a righteousness of my own that comes from the law, but that which is through faith in Christ—the righteousness that comes from God and is by faith"* (Phil. 3:9).

The apostle Paul came to the point in his relationship with Jesus that he considered the things of this world rubbish in comparison to the riches of knowing Jesus. There was no comparison as far as he was concerned. He didn't mourn the loss of the things of the world. Everything paled in light of the glory of God. This is what the Church must point people toward. We're not called to merely "be friends" with those outside of Christ. We are called to love them, and a vital part of loving them is bringing them to the knowledge of eternal life in Jesus. Life is messy and we are weak, but God's glory is all around us in spite of us.

REFLECTION QUESTIONS

1. What is the righteousness of God?

_____

2. How do we, as part of the Church, point people toward knowledge of eternal life in Christ?

_____

3. When Rolland says that we are pilgrims and strangers on the earth, camping deep in enemy territory, what is this enemy territory he is talking about?

_____

Session Ten

TRUE HOLINESS

Rolland Baker

"Since we have these promises, dear friends, let us purify ourselves from everything that contaminates body and spirit, perfecting holiness out of reverence for God."
—2 Corinthians 7:1

SESSION SUMMARY

God has a message for the world, and He wants to convey that message through us, the Church. His message centers on Jesus Christ and the love and joy that Jesus embodies. When we are able to understand and participate in the Christian life with true love and joy, we are well equipped to carry out the Great Commission. When we are joyful about who God is and what He has done for us and when we love like Jesus loves, our hearts are equipped to be the kind of holy and set-apart people God wants in the world. The world sees God through us as we embody His holy character. As we go out, genuinely full of the joy and love of heaven, others are able to recognize the authenticity they hunger for and can more easily embrace what God so generously gives.

One aspect of the authentic Christian life is learning to live with freedom in the Spirit. Manifestations of the Spirit are surprising and disturbing to some, but they are nothing new. They can be found throughout the history of the Church. We need to become comfortable with the manifestations that come with God's presence if we are to swim in the mighty river of God that brings the revival the world desperately needs.

Authentic Christian missions training begins with the task of preparing our inner self first as a firm foundation for the "nuts and bolts" of missiology that are to follow. We must allow God to conform our inner person through the process of consecration. This inner transformation is possible because God's Spirit will give us the desire, willingness, and power to set our life apart and dedicate it to Him. **We must do the hard work of inner preparation lest we fall into the trap of trying to build a foundation on a combination of our carnal nature and God's divine nature.** This kind of a foundation will not withstand the storms of the enemy. We must earnestly pursue the person of Jesus Christ, who is Holiness, until His holiness overtakes our sinfulness and transforms us into a people ready to do His will.

MAIN CONCEPTS FROM SESSION TEN

*"Since we have these promises, dear friends, let us purify ourselves from everything
that contaminates body and spirit, perfecting holiness out of reverence for God."*
—2 Corinthians 7:1

TRUE HOLINESS

Rolland Baker

God's Message to the World: *"Therefore my heart is glad and my glory rejoices; my flesh also will dwell securely."* —Psalm 16:9 NASB

- We are called to be joyful about who God is and what He has done for us.

- We are called to love like Jesus.

- When we understand and participate in these two things, all other aspects of the Great Commission will naturally follow.

- Every Christian has the ability to be used by God for signs and wonders, both inside and outside the walls of the church.

- Jesus is our model for this kind of "Great Commission" lifestyle.

- A "Great Commission" lifestyle is to be one of the main points of the Christian life, but we cannot get there outside of intimacy with God.

A Holy God: *"For it is written: 'Be holy, because I am holy.'"* —1 Peter 1:16

- In the Bible, God emphasizes holiness as the most important aspect of His character.

- God is distinct and distinguished from all else and He wants us to be the same. We are sanctified believers, reflecting the holiness of Jesus. *"We have been set apart as holy because Jesus Christ did what God wanted Him to do by sacrificing His body once and for all"* (Heb. 10:10 GW).

- Worldly success is nothing without the character of Jesus in our hearts. *"My prayer is not that You take them out of the world but that You protect them from the evil one. They are not of the world, even as I am not of it"* (John 17:15-16).

Freedom in the Spirit: *"There is a river whose streams make glad the city of God, the holy place where the Most High dwells."* —Psalm 46:4

- Freedom in the Spirit comes at a price.

- Jesus paid that price. Now all we have to do is appropriate what is ours to receive.

- When we have true freedom in the Spirit we are not put off by the different manifestations that come upon us when the power of God touches us.

- These manifestations can be found throughout the history of the Church.

- Negative impressions of holiness make it difficult to understand true holiness.

Build the Foundation First: *"For no one can lay any foundation other than the one already laid, which is Jesus Christ."* —1 Corinthians 3:11

- In order to prepare yourself for the mission field, focus on your own inner healing and holiness issues first.

- Once your interior life is solid, the outworkings of missions can be built on that solid foundation.

- Don't build a foundation on a combination of carnal and divine nature.

- Submit your carnal nature to the cleansing of the Holy Spirit and build only on His divine nature.

  But I am afraid that just as Eve was deceived by the serpent's cunning, your minds may somehow be led astray from your sincere and pure devotion to Christ. For if someone comes to you and preaches a Jesus other than the Jesus we preached, or if you receive a different spirit from the one you received, or a different gospel from the one you accepted, you put up with it easily enough (2 Corinthians 11:3-4).

- Stand on the rock that is Jesus Christ. In this way you will not be easily swayed.

God Is Going to Make You Perfect: *"To him who is able to keep you from falling and to present you before his glorious presence without fault and with great joy."* —Jude 1:24

- God is able to make us perfect so that we will be ready for Him to present us before the throne without spot or wrinkle.

- Sabbath rest is how we get our inner self ready to receive from God; it is part of His design for His people. *"And God blessed the seventh day and made it holy"* (Gen. 2:3).

- In order to receive God's Sabbath rest you must consecrate yourself—declare yourself dedicated to God's divine purpose; keep His decrees.

- In the power of His Spirit He will give us a willingness and a desire and the ability to be set apart and dedicated to Him.

Holiness: Our Most Exciting Goal: *"I will accept you as fragrant incense when I bring you out from the nations and gather you from the countries where you have been scattered, and I will show Myself holy among you in the sight of the nations."* —Ezekiel 20:41

- Holiness and the heart of Jesus are one and the same. All knowledge, all wisdom, all perfection, all joy, all excellence, all purity—all those things are not abstract ideas. They are embodied in the person of Jesus Christ. Jesus has become our wisdom, our sanctification, in whom are all the treasures of wisdom and knowledge (see 1 Cor. 1:30).

- Make every effort to live in peace with everyone and to be holy; without holiness, no one will see the Lord (see Heb. 12:14).

- When we consecrate ourselves to Him, pressing in to His holiness, God is our reward.

Session Ten Devotions

GOD'S MESSAGE TO THE WORLD

"Therefore my heart is glad and my glory rejoices; my flesh also will dwell securely."
—Psalm 16:9 NASB

Upon his conversion to Christianity, Pastor John Wimber, one of the founding leaders of the Vineyard Movement, began to attend church and read the Bible. His time in the Word led him to understand that we have been commissioned to heal the sick, raise the dead, cleanse the lepers, and set the captives free. Wimber would refer to this spiritual mandate as "doin' the stuff." He believed that every Christian believer has the ability to be used by God for signs and wonders, both inside and outside the walls of the church, with Jesus as our model. Wimber understood the Great Commission to be one of the main points of the Christian life, while also emphasizing intimacy with God. Wimber's teachings have strongly influenced neo-charismatic evangelical Christian denominations worldwide. But in spite of this influence, many in the Church are still confused about the point of the Christian life.

Is it our job to go to a ministry school and learn how to do the miraculous, the supernatural, and if so what is the point? What are we to be doing as followers of Jesus? Do we do the stuff," and what does that look like? Are we to get out and evangelize as much as possible? Certainly, Jesus did tell His disciples to do those things, and we do them, but what is the point of doing all of this? What is the point of the Church? What is the Church trying to do? Is it trying to fix the world, to design new wineskins to hold the latter-days revival, to get a Bible into the hands of every person on earth? Is the Church trying to climb the seven mountains of world culture, to take dominion over the earth, or are we just trying to turn everybody into Christians? What is our life as believers actually about? What message does the Church have for the world?

These are all valid questions. Different people within the Church will answer these questions in different ways, but as I ponder them two things clearly stand out. **We are called to be joyful about who God is and what He has done for us, and we are called to love Jesus, and everyone else as we love Him.** If we can understand and participate in these two aspects of the Christian life, then I believe the rest of the Great Commission will fall into place naturally.

REFLECTION QUESTIONS

1. How would you answer the question, "What message does the Church have for the world?"

_____
_____
_____
_____
_____
_____
_____
_____
_____

2. How do joy and love impact every aspect of the Great Commission?

_____
_____
_____
_____
_____
_____
_____
_____
_____
_____
_____
_____
_____
_____
_____

3. What aspects of "doin' the stuff" are you uncomfortable with and why?

_____
_____
_____
_____
_____
_____
_____
_____
_____
_____
_____

A HOLY GOD

"For it is written: 'Be holy, because I am holy.'"
—1 PETER 1:16

A lot of preaching in the Church today assumes that God wants us prosperous and healed; He wants our families whole and wants us to be successful at our careers and to be blessed on this earth and favored and anointed, but there is no discussion about what dreams and successes are good and which ones are not. If God is just all about success, what does that mean for each one of us? You can be an excellent surgeon and a really awful person. You can be a famous scientist and be consumed by jealousy. There were two very famous scientists and mathematicians who simultaneously invented calculus. But sadly, for the remainder of their lives they fought each other to get credit for being the first to invent this valuable math. They were consumed by an obsession over their reputation, and one has to ask, "To what end?" They were successful as world-famous mathematicians, but fell short when it came to character.

What about the character of God? How does He want to be perceived? What does God want to be known for? **A word search of the Bible reveals that, more than anything else, God wants to be known as holy.** He wants to be seen as holy through us, His people, and He wants to be known as the One who makes us holy (see Lev. 20:8). God could be known for a lot of things, but more than anything else, from the beginning in Scripture, God states that He wants to be known as holy. The Greek translation of *holy* is "set apart, sacred." In other words, God is distinct and distinguished from all else, and He intends for us to also be distinct and distinguished from the rest of the world. The writer of Hebrews says, *"We have been set apart as holy because Jesus Christ did what God wanted him to do by sacrificing his body once and for all"* (Heb. 10:10 GW).

As Jesus prays for His disciples before His crucifixion, He says, *"My prayer is not that you take them out of the world but that you protect them from the evil one. They are not of the world, even as I am not of it"* (John 17:15-16). As sanctified believers, we are set apart, reflecting the holiness of our Lord and Savior. Although God is more than able to defend His reputation, when the world sees us as "set apart," they can more easily understand the holiness of God. When they see us genuinely full of the joy and love of heaven, they are able to recognize the authenticity they have been hungering for and more easily embrace what God so generously gives.

REFLECTION QUESTIONS

1. How would you complete the sentence, "God's desire for us to succeed means…"?

_____
_____
_____
_____
_____
_____
_____

2. How do you feel about being holy and set apart?

_____
_____
_____
_____
_____
_____
_____
_____
_____
_____
_____
_____
_____

3. What does "in the world, but not of the world" mean to you?

_____
_____
_____
_____
_____
_____
_____
_____
_____
_____
_____

FREEDOM IN THE SPIRIT

"There is a river whose streams make glad the city of God,
the holy place where the Most High dwells."
—Psalm 46:4

The first time Heidi and I were in Toronto, our reputation was at stake. We stood to lose a considerably large portion of our financial support just for being there. Because of this, we were sitting in the back trying to hide while everybody else was up front manifesting. Suddenly, John Arnott stood up and said, "Is there anyone here from Mozambique?" The next thing we knew, we're up front and Heidi's on the carpet and all these television cameras are broadcasting nationally Heidi Baker on the carpet, swimming like a flounder on the bottom of the river. Her mouth was going like a fish. She couldn't believe later what she did. For those of you who know Heidi, she is the poster child of wild, crazy, and embarrassing manifestations. Sometimes on TV interviews she looks so correct and together, but when God touches her all that goes out the window.

There was so much that flowed out of Toronto into our stream, but the big picture is actually much broader. Most of what went on in Toronto was seen by my grandfather eighty years prior in China. He baptized ten thousand people in the mountain rivers of Southwest China who had been taught nothing about revival or manifestations or the Holy Spirit or any of that. They would come out of the water, eighty years ago, rolling on the ground, speaking in eight languages, laughing their heads off, caught up in visions of heaven, unable to walk or talk for days. Many were transported in the Spirit to other locations. What happened at Toronto was not new.

What happened in China and Toronto and what is still happening all over the globe is a picture of freedom in the Holy Spirit. **One dip of your toe into the mighty river of God's Spirit and everything changes**. Some people go ankle deep, some knee deep, and some just dive in and flounder at the bottom. There are those who say that the Renewal Movement is a reaction against uptight, legalistic, controlling church environments that are so rigid that true holiness has a hard time gaining a foothold, and as a result it gets a bad reputation. The excesses of the movement have created a negative impression of holiness, making it difficult for many to understand what true holiness means.

Freedom in the Spirit comes at a price. Jesus paid the price so that all you have to do is dip your toe in His mighty river. In the midst of messy ministry that is littered with our human weaknesses, revival can still occur, to the glory of God!

REFLECTION QUESTIONS

1. How far into the river are you *really* willing to go, and for what purpose?

2. How would you respond to negative reactions from people in your life if you were to experience wild, crazy, and embarrassing manifestations?

3. What price are you willing to pay for true freedom in the Spirit?

BUILD THE FOUNDATION FIRST

"For no one can lay any foundation other than the one already laid, which is Jesus Christ."
—1 Corinthians 3:11

The bulk of mission training available today focuses on communication methods and ways of learning language and immersing yourself in the culture. You'll find missionary methods and strategies, computerized models of mission fields, and what techniques work and don't work. This is because it is a lot easier to preach about money, how to control return, blessings, prosperity, even healing, and a lot more difficult to talk about things of the heart such as holiness. But when you go deep into heart issues and find God's answers, all the rest will flow out of that knowledge. If you concentrate on building your inner foundations first, the outworkings will naturally follow.

Most of us don't wake up in the morning and say, "I just want to be holy today." We tend not to think about holiness too much, and that is unfortunate. The Christian life has a lot to do with holiness. Joy has to do with holiness. Supernatural gifts of the Spirit have to do with holiness. Evangelism has to do with holiness. Can one be a learned missiologist and not understand holiness? **If God's holiness sets Him apart and sets us apart, then shouldn't our aim as missionaries be to be set apart?** What does it look like to be set apart in the mission field?

Many of you using this material are in one of Iris's Harvest Schools, and many of you are not. Many of you are somewhere around the globe and you have a desire to go into missions and you want to know how Iris does missions. The way we do missions at Iris is different from the world and from worldly organizations and corporations and even a lot of other Christian organizations. We don't claim our way to be the "right" way or the only way; we only know how God directs us and what works for us. We build the foundation first and then watch the rest follow in the power of the Spirit. Life in our particular mission field is so fiercely challenging that going forward without a foundation is not optional for us.

In First Corinthians 3:10, Paul, by the grace of God, speaks as a wise master builder entreating us not to try and build on a foundation that is a combination of carnal and divine nature. We have been given Christ, the Rock, upon whom we are to build. All else is sinking sand. In his second letter to the Corinthians, Paul goes on to warn us of what happens to those without a firm foundation in Jesus Christ:

> *But I am afraid that just as Eve was deceived by the serpent's cunning, your minds may somehow be led astray from your sincere and pure devotion to Christ. For if someone comes to you and preaches a Jesus other than the Jesus we preached, or if you receive a different spirit from the one you received, or a different gospel from the one you accepted, you put up with it easily enough* (2 Corinthians 11:3-4).

How easily we are swayed if our feet aren't on solid ground! We must do the hard work of building our inner foundation so that our feet can stand when all around us is demonic chaos. On the rock of Christ, God will build His church, and the gates of hell will not prevail against it.

REFLECTION QUESTIONS

1. At this point in your life, how have you gone about the difficult work of building your inner foundation on Jesus Christ?

   _____

   _____

   _____

   _____

   _____

   _____

   _____

   _____

2. Specifically, what does it look like to you to be "set apart" in the mission field?

   _____

   _____

   _____

   _____

   _____

   _____

   _____

   _____

3. In Ephesians 2:21, what is Paul talking about when he says, *"In him the whole building is joined together and rises to become a holy temple in the Lord"*? What is the "whole building" composed of?

   _____

   _____

   _____

   _____

   _____

   _____

   _____

GOD IS GOING TO MAKE YOU PERFECT

*"To Him who is able to keep you from falling and to present you
before His glorious presence without fault and with great."*
—Jude 24

God wants us to be serious about Sabbath rest. So serious that He brings it to our attention in the second chapter of Genesis: *"And God blessed the seventh day and made it holy"* (Gen. 2:3). God's rest is a *holy* time. He wants us to take one day out of each week and set it aside for Him, make it holy, and in so doing He will make us holy. *"Keep My decrees and follow them. I am the Lord, who makes you holy"* (Lev. 20:8). In the Old Testament, Sabbath rest was a covenant arrangement between God and His people. In the New Testament, the Book of Hebrews tells us to be diligent to enter His rest because God provides His Sabbath rest for His people. Jesus died to give us this future rest in heaven. As soon as we leave this world and enter heaven, we'll never have to work again!

But let's return to the Old Testament for a minute and examine more closely the issue of Sabbath rest and how we get our inner self ready to receive such a gift. Leviticus 20:7 says, *"Consecrate yourselves and be holy, because I am the Lord your God."* Then in the next verse, another perspective is introduced: *"Keep my decrees and follow them. I am the Lord, who makes you holy."* First God says that we are to consecrate ourselves and then He says He will make us holy. So which is it? Philippians 2:12-13 says, *"Work out your salvation with fear and trembling, for it is God who works in you to will and to act according to His good pleasure.* Once again we are faced with different perspectives in the dichotomy that is part of the kingdom.

If God makes us holy, how then will we experience that holiness? Scripture tells us that we will experience His holiness as a desire and willingness and ability to consecrate ourselves. He'll give us the desire and willingness and power to work out our salvation with fear and trembling. If you don't want to work out your salvation with fear and trembling and you don't want to consecrate yourself, what does that show God? That He hasn't made you holy yet!

One of the great things about the Christian life is that we never have to pretend. We don't have to pretend we are perfect. We're not holy until we're holy, and we can be perfectly honest with God about that because He knows it already. Even though God sees us through the blood of Jesus, I want Him to see every little thing that is wrong with me so that He can fix it. Who wants a God who says, "Oh, don't worry about it. I can't see your faults, so what is there to worry about?" The exciting thing about the Christian life is not that you're going to make money or gain power or find yourself with a strong anointing or have a mega-church. **The exciting thing about the Christian life is that God is going to make you perfect**. He is able to finish what He began in you and present you before the throne on that great day without spot, fault, or wrinkle and with great joy in His presence (see Jude 24).

REFLECTION QUESTIONS

1. Why is it important to enter into Sabbath rest?

_____

_____

_____

_____

_____

_____

_____

2. How have you been working out your salvation with fear and trembling?

_____

_____

_____

_____

_____

_____

_____

3. Why doesn't God make us perfect here on earth?

_____

_____

_____

_____

_____

_____

_____

HOLINESS: OUR MOST EXCITING GOAL

"I will accept you as fragrant incense when I bring you out from the nations
and gather you from the countries where you have been scattered, and
I will show Myself holy among you in the sight of the nations."
—Ezekiel 20:41

I didn't like the idea of holiness very much growing up in church. It seemed so impersonal. Holiness sounded dry and not fun at all. Gradually, as I grew in my faith I began to realize that holiness is not impersonal. It's not a set of ideals or goals. Holiness is the person of Jesus Christ. The New Testament says, *"Jesus has become our wisdom sent from God, our approval, our holiness, and our ransom from sin"* (1 Cor. 1:30 GW). All knowledge, all wisdom, all perfection, all joy, all excellence, all purity—all those things are not abstract ideas. They are embodied in the person of Jesus Christ. He personifies holiness. If you have Jesus, you have holiness, and if you have holiness, you have Jesus. Holiness is where all the excitement and energy and the power and the glory of being alive are found. If you set your heart on holiness, you have set your heart on Jesus because the two are one and the same.

What could be better than being made holy by God until you are exactly what He likes? If you knew that you were exactly what God likes, that would be the end of all jealousy, all competition, all striving, all worry, all stress. All you need to know is that you are exactly what God wants; then you won't care if someone else is ten times prettier or smarter than you if you are exactly what He wants. Hebrews 12 makes holiness the deal of a lifetime: *"Make every effort to live in peace with all men and to be holy; without holiness no one will see the Lord"* (Heb. 12:14).

REFLECTION QUESTIONS

1. What do you think about having holiness as your most exciting goal?

_____

_____

_____

_____

_____

_____

_____

_____

_____

_____

_____

_____

_____

_____

2. What do you think of Rolland's statement that the happiest people on earth are the holiest?

_____

_____

_____

_____

_____

_____

_____

_____

_____

_____

_____

_____

_____

3. How are holiness and Jesus one and the same?

_____

_____

_____

_____

_____

_____

_____

_____

_____

_____

_____

_____

Part Three

YOUR ASSIGNMENT

TENDERNESS AND COMPASSION

Heidi Baker

*"But thanks be to God, who always leads us in triumphal procession in Christ
and through us spreads everywhere the fragrance of the knowledge of Him."*
—2 CORINTHIANS 2:14

SESSION SUMMARY

In order to freely give what we have so freely received, we need to know Jesus. If we are going to become radical, laid-down lovers of God who walk the earth like Jesus did, we need to know how He walked, how He talked, what He "ate" to nourish His spirit. Much of this "knowing" begins in His Word, the Bible. To appropriate our royal, heavenly DNA we must marinate in the Word. We must understand what it is that we must lay down so that Jesus can pick us up. We need to stop eating spiritual junk food and start feasting on the Bread of Life. Spiritually malnourished believers become easy prey for the enemy who roams like a ravenous lion.

The Holy Spirit's job is to reveal the Father and the Son to us. When we have fellowship with the Holy Spirit, we align ourselves to unite with Christ so that we may reach out and take hold of all of the attributes of His character. Tenderness and compassion, joy and love are ours in Jesus. He is calling us to come up higher, to come into His presence and receive the full measure of Him. Fellowship with Him will bring all the riches of His kingdom to bear on any situation we find ourselves in. This fellowship is not a one-time event. We need His fullness in us every day. We need to constantly go back and wade in the River of Life if we are to be life givers, speaking the language of heaven. But, to learn this heavenly language we must spend time with the one who speaks it—Jesus Christ Himself. Know your identity, spend time in the Word, become intimate with Jesus, and watch how God moves through you. Thanks be to God, who leads us in His triumph, for we are the sweet aroma of Christ to those who are being saved and those who are perishing!

MAIN CONCEPTS FROM SESSION ELEVEN

"But thanks be to God, who always leads us in triumphal procession in Christ and through us spreads everywhere the fragrance of the knowledge of Him."
—2 Corinthians 2:14

TENDERNESS AND COMPASSION

Heidi Baker

The One Who Is Worthy: *"Freely you have received, freely give."* —Matthew 10:8

- We "follow" the Lamb who was slain as disciples, sitting at His feet.

- The reward of Jesus' suffering, purchased by His blood, is the cleansing of His people, the Church, which is His bride.

- How do we walk like Jesus walked on the earth?

- We study the Scriptures, particularly the gospels.

- We understand our identity—who we are in Christ.

- We give ourselves totally to Jesus.

- Knowing your royal identity in Christ means that you have free access to the One who is worthy, but it also means that you must live with your hands wide open, giving it all away.

The Bread of Life: *"I am the living bread that came down from heaven. If anyone eats of this bread, he will live forever. This bread is My flesh, which I will give for the life of the world."* —John 6:51

- The mature in Christ eat the "bread of heaven," not spiritual junk food.

- Jesus is the bread of heaven, and we can feast on Him through His Word and when we spend time with Him.

- Spiritually malnourished Christians are easy prey for the enemy.

- We can be physically healthy and spiritually malnourished.

- Time spent in worship and praise brings the divine presence of Christ.

- His divine presence washes us clean and causes the seeds He has planted in us to bear fruit in season.

Is Jesus Your Savior?: *"If you have any encouragement from being united with Christ, if any comfort from His love, if any fellowship with the Spirit, if any tenderness and compassion, then make my joy complete by being like-minded, having the same love, being one in spirit and purpose."* —Philippians 2:1-2

- Give up your culture to live in the culture of Jesus.

- Become His slave and receive His freedom so that you can give it away.

- Let Jesus open your "blind" eyes and your "deaf" ears.

- He will make your "lame" legs walk with the shoes of peace and the message of the Gospel.

- He will bring His life to all the dead places in you.

- With Jesus as your Savior, all things are possible.

Fellowship with the Holy Spirit: *"If you have any encouragement from being united with Christ, if any comfort from His love, if any fellowship with the Spirit, if any tenderness and compassion, then make my joy complete by being like-minded, having the same love, being one in spirit and purpose. Do nothing out of selfish ambition or vain conceit, but in humility consider others better than yourselves."* —Philippians 2:1–3

- Fellowship with Jesus will bring all the riches of His kingdom to bear on any situation.

- Be encouraged through union with Christ; be comforted by His love.

- Share in in the things of His Spirit; embrace His tenderness and compassion.

- Fellowship with Jesus will make your joy complete.

Do Nothing Out of Selfish Ambition: *"Your attitude should be the same as that of Christ Jesus."* —Philippians 2:5

- Serving like Jesus brings life and light.

- Selfish ambition is thinking you and your needs are more important than others and their needs. *"Do nothing out of selfish ambition or vain conceit, but in humility consider others better than yourselves"* (Phil. 2:3).

- Jesus never lived out of selfish ambition. *"Who, being in very nature God, did not consider equality with God something to be grasped"* (Phil. 2:6).

Session Eleven Devotions

THE ONE WHO IS WORTHY

"Freely you have received, freely give."
—MATTHEW 10:8

We really are precious sons and daughters of the most holy high King of heaven, but what does that mean as you follow the Lamb who was slain? What does that mean as you're called to bring in the reward of His suffering? God called you because He loves you. To be a radical lover of God is to walk like Jesus on the earth. What does it look like to walk like Jesus on the earth? You have to ask Him every day what it looks like because how are you going to know if you don't spend time with Him? It is in the secret place with Him that you'll find your daily bread, the manna from heaven that feeds you on your journey.

Some of you reading this today are ready to be radical lovers of God. Like Joseph, you are ready to shave your head and wear the earring in order to accomplish God's will. You are ready to lay down your life so that He can pick it up. You are going to the nations, carrying the Gospel because you know the One who is worthy. You understand that Jesus gave His life for us, and your response is to give your life for Him. The mission field in Mozambique is so challenging that my flesh cries out to leave at times but thanks be to God, I know the One who is worthy and I stay. Every day I take hold of more of God and give my life in greater measure. That is my choice. Many in this generation struggle with a spirit of entitlement, thinking you can have it all, that there's no suffering involved in the Gospel. You are quick to retreat when there is a cost involved. If that is you, then don't head into the mission field.

Royalty is your DNA from heaven, and in order to steward that inheritance you must live as a bond slave to Christ. You must understand what it means to become nothing, following in the footsteps of Jesus, giving yourself totally to Him and allowing Him to choose your time and your season. Choosing to give everything to Jesus is not about a poverty spirit. When He is our all in all, we are rich beyond measure. Knowing your royal identity in Christ means that you have free access to the One who is worthy, but it also means that you must live with your hands wide open, giving it all away. When we freely give to the One who is worthy, we receive all that we need and more for this life and the next.

REFLECTION QUESTIONS

1. What is the reward of Jesus' suffering that we are called to bring in?

_____

_____

_____

2. Read Genesis 39–47. How did Joseph navigate life in a godless culture and still hold on to his faith?

3. What is a poverty spirit?

4. How can we be rich and poor at the same time?

THE BREAD OF LIFE

"I am the living bread that came down from heaven. If anyone eats of this bread, he will live forever. This bread is My flesh, which I will give for the life of the world."
—John 6:51

The mature in Christ don't spend time eating spiritual "cotton candy" and drinking spiritual "Diet Coke." God has given us His bread from heaven—Jesus Christ—and we are to eat that which is good, the bread from heaven that sustains us. Without it, there is no life. All else is "junk food." We must be people who feast on the Word of God, allowing it to sink into our spirits and nourish us.

In the Word, we will come to know Jesus, but beware—little sound bits and bites of the Word aren't enough. You need the full meal in order to have the proper nourishment to sustain you. The enemy never rests. He roams like a lion, looking for the weak. Those who feast on spiritual junk food or take just a little bit of Scripture here and a little bite there will find themselves easy prey. Let the Word of God get inside of you every day. Read the Bible, listen to the Bible on audio, do whatever works for you to be fully nourished in the Spirit.

Many of you are first-world Westerners living in a culture that is heavily focused on the "best" nourishment for your body. You eat the best organic foods and take expensive supplements. Your bodies are well-nourished, but your spirits are suffering from malnutrition. Here in Mozambique we eat a lot of rice and beans. Once in a while we get a piece of chicken to go with our rice and beans, and we consider that a really good meal. Our bodies may not be the most well-nourished on the planet, but our spirits are overflowing with good health. We worship every day, with abandon, on our faces in the dirt, giving it all to the One who is worthy of it all. Jesus comes and walks among us, His river of living water washing away the grime of the world and causing all things to become new. Seeds sprout and bear fruit in this living water, and the joy and love of Jesus becomes our daily fresh bread. We are able to follow Him wholeheartedly, not looking to the left or to the right, because we feed on the meat of the Gospel.

REFLECTION QUESTIONS

1. Are you eating spiritual junk food or feasting on manna from heaven?

---

2. Read Deuteronomy 28:14. How difficult is it for you to "stay on the path"?

3. Hebrews 5:13-14 says, *"Anyone who lives on milk, being still an infant, is not acquainted with the teaching about righteousness. But solid food is for the mature, who by constant use have trained themselves to distinguish good from evil."* How does this passage equate to the concept of spiritual nourishment versus spiritual malnourishment?

IS JESUS YOUR SAVIOR?

"If you have any encouragement from being united with Christ, if any comfort from His love, if any fellowship with the Spirit, if any tenderness and compassion, then make my joy complete by being like-minded, having the same love, being one in spirit and purpose."
—Philippians 2:1-2

Are you united with Christ? Is He your Savior and your God? Is He your all in all? Do you love Him more than the very breath of life? Do you know that He is so in love with you? He loves you beyond what you can ever imagine. It's true! And He wants the best for you. If you find any comfort from His love, receive it right now, today, wherever you are. He wants to comfort all of us in His love, to come and give us a big hug. Jesus is absolutely in love with you, and when He calls you to give your life away and shave your head and put on the earring (see Gen. 41:14), it's because He loves you so much that you get the privilege of receiving that which sets us free. You choose to become a slave in order to bring freedom. This is the greatest freedom on earth, the greatest privilege.

Constant communion with the living God of the universe who loves us with an everlasting love brings us comfort, tenderness, and compassion that takes us to a place of overflowing joy so that, like the Moravians, we will gladly sell ourselves into slavery so that others might be free. This is the reality of missions. In the mission field you will give up your "culture" to live in His culture. Kingdom culture is radically different from any other culture. In kingdom culture, the blind see, the deaf hear, the lame walk, and the dead are raised. I'm not just talking about those we minister to. I'm talking about our blind eyes seeing, our deaf ears opening, our lame legs walking for the Gospel, our "deadness" giving way to life in the Spirit! When Jesus is your Savior, all this is possible and more!

REFLECTION QUESTIONS

1. How much are you ready to give up your "culture" to live in His culture? What is your "culture"?

----

2. How much "deadness" is there still in you?

3. How would you explain to someone what it means to have Jesus as your Savior?

FELLOWSHIP WITH THE HOLY SPIRIT

"If you have any encouragement from being united with Christ, if any comfort from His love, if any fellowship with the Spirit, if any tenderness and compassion, then make my joy complete by being like-minded, having the same love, being one in spirit and purpose. Do nothing out of selfish ambition or vain conceit, but in humility consider others better than yourselves."
—Philippians 2:1–3

Whatever you do in this world, let it be done full of love. Remember that you are called to fellowship with the Holy Spirit and you need to learn His language. People ask me how long it took to learn Portuguese. I tell them I'm still learning. Whenever I go to a country where there's another language, I'm learning. Until I go home to Jesus I'll be learning. I'm still learning the language of Jesus, which is tenderness, compassion, and kindness. When I speak this language I make His joy complete.

Too often I have found myself struggling to speak in the "appropriate" language when I'm in difficult circumstances. My carnal nature wants to blurt out something inappropriate in one language, while my spirit knows that I need to speak in the language of heaven. I recall one particular meeting with local government officials. They had just informed me that after eleven years our Bible school was still not properly registered. As we sat there in the school building with sunlight streaming in through nail holes in the roof that wasn't supposed to be there according to the officials, I felt my inappropriate language trying to take over. Then I heard the Lord say, "Just be quiet, Heidi. Just listen and trust." As I began to listen to His voice I heard tenderness and compassion. He was calling me to show His light at that moment, to prefer those who sat in front of me over myself. "Call them up," He said. "Call them up! You stand up and shine and show them what it looks like." Looking them in the eyes I said, "I believe in you. I trust you. I believe that God has anointed you for this day, for this moment, for this meeting, and I trust in you, and I bless you to be thoroughly anointed and qualified for that which God has given you today." As God's tenderness and compassion flowed over them, their eyes began to change. The kingdom of God came into the room and changed everything because I was willing to be one in spirit and of one mind with Jesus. Fellowship with Him will bring all the riches of His kingdom to bear on any situation.

REFLECTION QUESTIONS

1. How much are you able to fellowship with the Holy Spirit in the middle of difficult circumstances?

2. Why is it that we who have walked closely with God for so many years, still have to battle our will versus His will?

3. What kind of encouragement do you receive from being united with Christ?

DO NOTHING OUT OF SELFISH AMBITION

"Your attitude should be the same as that of Christ Jesus."
—Philippians 2:5

King Jesus, the Son of God, the Savior of the world, equal with God in every way, came with abject humility, fully knowing who He was, always knowing who He was, never doubting who He was, and He made himself nothing, not considering equality with God something to be grasped. King Jesus—whose streets are paved with gold and whose gates are made of pearls and diamonds and rubies and emeralds, this matchless King of Glory with riches beyond anything we've ever seen or imagined, the One who has access to everything—laid it all down for the sake of love. He emptied Himself, became a servant, made in human likeness, the King of kings and the Lord of lords, who dances on the streets of gold. He went into the womb of a woman, became a human being, and nursed at an adopted mother's breast. He crawled around in the dirt and walked and listened and learned what humility looks like. This is what missions is about. It's you knowing your identity, knowing you have the right to absolutely everything, and choosing to become a servant, choosing to become like King Jesus—a bond slave, a servant who is a beloved child of God.

"Do nothing out of selfish ambition or vain conceit, but in humility consider others better than yourselves" (Phil. 2:3). There are days when I want to forget these words from Philippians. I want to complain because someone took all the water, ate all the peanut butter. I want to complain about the boney fish and having no more eggs. I want to tell someone that I just don't feel like doing this anymore. And then the Holy Spirit reminds me that it's not about me. I have to consider the government officials who keep coming against us better than myself. When they deport 45 people for no reason I have to consider them better. I need Jesus. I need His language. I need His heart. I need His presence and His grace and His joy and His love. I need all of Him, every day.

In the midst of my frustration I remember that no one should live on a shredded rag of a mat. No one should live in a smoldering garbage dump. No one should be beaten, raped, orphaned. It's not about me. It's about Him. It's about what Jesus has to give. It's about what is in His heart, what is on His lips. We have been called to shine like heaven's stars in the very darkest places. He wants us to carry *His* Word of life. It's not our light that pierces the darkness. It's not our word that brings life. He's the One. He's so beautiful. He's so lovely. He's worthy. What else can we do but give our everything to Him?

REFLECTION QUESTIONS

1. Why is identity so important to the laid-down life that Jesus calls us to?

_____
_____
_____
_____
_____
_____
_____
_____

2. How many of your relationships are characterized by the mindset of Christ Jesus?

_____
_____
_____
_____
_____
_____
_____
_____
_____
_____
_____
_____

3. How do you define selfish ambition?

_____
_____
_____
_____
_____
_____
_____
_____
_____
_____
_____

Session Twelve

WORK FROM A PLACE OF REST

Rolland Baker

"And behold, there arose a great storm on the sea, so that the boat was being covered with the waves; but Jesus Himself was asleep."
—Matthew 8:24 NASB

SESSION SUMMARY

Every good and perfect gift is from above, coming down from the Father of the heavenly lights, who does not change like shifting shadows (James 1:17).

It is difficult for many Christians to understand what it means to "work" from a place of "rest." The two are mutually exclusive, but not in the kingdom of God. The more we learn to rest in Him, the more He can accomplish His will. Notice that it doesn't say "the more *we* can accomplish His will." It's not about us accomplishing anything. But how do we get into this place of rest with God? Is it something we have to work at? In a sense, yes, we have to work at understanding several things about our self and about God in order to understand His rest.

Perhaps you've noticed by now that everything about our relationship with God begins with the heart. There's no way around it—each one of us needs "heart surgery" at the hands of the Great Physician before we're fit to put our hand to the plow. Radical heart surgery involves allowing God to repair those things in your heart that are broken or damaged so that your heart can function as God intends. Full heart-to-heart union with God can't happen when our hearts are in need of repair. If you have a hole in your tire, it's going to need repair before it can drive smoothly. Likewise, when the devil shoots holes in our heart, you need God to repair things before you can run smoothly again, in tandem with Him.

But why love God so much? Why should we be eager to enter into a place of divine love with God? These are certainly important questions to ask and the answers lead us straight to Jesus, which is precisely where God wants us. **The Christian life begins with Jesus and never ends because of Him.** Because of Jesus, our sins are forgiven—we are set free from sin that enslaves us. But to be set free, we must understand that something is keeping us bound, and that something is our sin. God so desires that we be free from sin that He gave His best—His Son Jesus, to die free of sin so that we might live free of sin. We must understand this foundational aspect of the Gospel in order to come into divine relationship with God. Understanding is the first step to a life of freedom in Christ.

An unencumbered life of freedom in Christ has a specific composition to it. It involves complete surrender to God's will, which is in part a leap of faith and part understanding that His good and perfect will is far better than our will. It also involves confronting the reality that we are all sinners on equal footing before the cross, equally in need of God's grace and mercy and fully and completely loved by our good and perfect God. Because He is completely trustworthy, we can completely trust Him. It is from this place of trust that we can move from striving in our own will to resting in His will.

MAIN CONCEPTS FROM SESSION TWELVE

"And behold, there arose a great storm on the sea, so that the boat was being covered with the waves; but Jesus Himself was asleep."
—Matthew 8:24 NASB

WORK FROM A PLACE OF REST

Rolland Baker

Surprised by God: *"Then I heard the voice of the Lord saying, 'Whom shall I send? And who will go for Us?' And I said, 'Here am I. Send me!'"* —Isaiah 6:8

- We don't have to worry about hearing God's voice.

- God will always make sure we hear Him when He has something to say. We just need to listen and obey. *"For He is our God, and we are the people of His pasture and the sheep of His hand. Today, if you would hear His voice, do not harden your hearts"* (Ps. 95:7-8 NASB).

Heart Surgery: *"The heart is deceitful above all things and beyond cure. Who can understand it?"* —Jeremiah 17:9

- Radical heart surgery is when God repairs those things in your heart that are broken or damaged so that your heart can function as He intends.

- Until your heart is "repaired" by God, your life will not be in full union with Him.

- God's "new wine" needs a new heart to flow through.

Why Love God?: *"We love because He first loved us."* —1 John 4:19

- It is easier to love God when we understand how much He loves us.

- God shows His great love for us through Jesus. *"And this same God who takes care of me will supply all your needs from His glorious riches, which have been given to us in Christ Jesus"* (Phil. 4:19 NLT).

- When we understand our sin, we can better understand the gift of God in Jesus.

Unencumbered Living: *"This is what the Lord says: 'Heaven is My throne, and the earth is My footstool. Where is the house you will build for Me? Where will My resting place be?'"* —Isaiah 66:1

- *The Mirror of Simple Souls*, a book by Marguerite Porete, examines several aspects of what a life given over to divine love looks like.

  - The first aspect is to understand that we can live a life free and unencumbered of things that hold us back from the fullness of a relationship with Him.

  - When we are joined to Jesus, we become one in spirit with Him. When we are one in spirit with Jesus, all striving ceases as His sovereign grace flows through us as pure love.

His Will: *"For I have come down from heaven not to do My will but to do the will of Him who sent Me."* —John 6:38

- The second aspect of a divine love relationship with God is learning how to completely surrender our will to God's will.

- Complete surrender to the will of God is scary until you realize that with complete surrender comes complete peace in the most difficult circumstances.

- Our dependence on God and our love for Him grows every day, making it easier and easier to surrender all to Him.

Our Sin Ever Before Us: *"For all have sinned and fall short of the glory of God."* —Romans 3:23

- The third aspect of a divine love relationship with God is understanding that our sins are not less than anyone else's, even the worst of sinners—the ground is level at the foot of the cross.

- We are as much in need of God's grace and mercy as the next person.

- We are all the worst of sinners and all the most loved by God.

- Jesus knows exactly who we are and that is precisely why He loves us so much.

Sweet Surrender: *"Why do you call Me good? No one is good except God alone."* —Mark 10:18 ESV

- The fourth aspect of a divine love relationship with God is His absolute goodness and perfection.

- Because God is perfect, it is impossible for Him to will anything other than that which is absolutely the best for you.

- Because of His absolute goodness, He is completely trustworthy, and because we can trust Him we can surrender all to Him.

Session Twelve Devotions

SURPRISED BY GOD

*"Then I heard the voice of the Lord saying, 'Whom shall I send? And
who will go for Us?' And I said, 'Here am I. Send me!'"*
—ISAIAH 6:8

In 1997, God sovereignly connected Mozambican pastor Surprise Sithole with Iris Ministries. Surprise is a man who loves Jesus more than life itself. His passion for his Savior has sent him to dark and unreached people groups with the message of the glory of God. Our remote bush outreach ministry came about in large part because we saw what God was doing with Surprise and felt led to partner with him. He is now International Director of Pastors for Iris, overseeing revival as it burns across Africa.

Surprise's story is like something out of the Book of Acts. The son of two witchdoctors, he was called by Jesus at the age of fifteen to leave his family and his old life behind. Surprise grew up poor and had never heard of Jesus, but when he heard the audible voice of the Lord he knew he was hearing someone speaking with authority, and so he obeyed. By the grace of God he was briefly mentored by a Christian who took him under his roof and shared the Gospel. From the moment Surprise heard of Jesus, his heart felt peace. Confessing Jesus as his Savior and armed with John 3:16 and little else, Surprise set off into the bush with the mighty message of Jesus. With no training and no knowledge of what he was supposed to be doing, Surprise was constantly surprised when people were healed as he prayed for them and shared the Good News.

When you ask Surprise about the night he heard God's voice, he will tell you that it wasn't a still, small voice. God's voice was loud and strong and carried great authority, coming with a sense of peace and security, unlike the experiences Surprise had with demonic spirits growing up. People worry about being able to hear God's voice, but God can speak when He wants to be heard. He is absolutely capable of making Himself heard. We just have to be willing to listen. When God spoke to Surprise for the first time, He told him to get up and leave his village immediately and never return or he would die. Later Surprise learned that his village had been attacked and many had died. If he had dismissed God's voice, he would have been among the casualties. **When God speaks, we must be willing to listen and obey.** We may be surprised by His presence, but we can be sure of one thing— He loves us and will lead us if we will only have the courage to follow. *"For He is our God, and we are the people of His pasture and the sheep of His hand. Today, if you would hear His voice, do not harden your hearts"* (Ps. 95:7-8 NASB).

REFLECTION QUESTIONS

1. How does Surprise Sithole's life illustrate Acts 10:34?

2. How do you recognize the voice of God when He is speaking to you?

3. What is the result of your obedience to God's voice?

HEART SURGERY

"The heart is deceitful above all things and beyond cure. Who can understand it?"
—JEREMIAH 17:9

In December of 2000, Iris put on a Christmas banquet at our Zimpeto center. We went out into the streets and called all the beggars. We went to the dump and called the destitute. We went to the brothels and called the prostitutes. We called the gangsters and drug addicts to come to God's banquet table. Heidi shopped for gifts for the children while our staff cooked diligently. On the day of the feast almost two hundred people came. We began with the wedding of a young couple and then we sang and danced with joy before the Lord.

Hearts changed at that wonderful banquet. One young man Heidi found on the streets turned from a violent street fighter into a radiant man of God. He went on to pastor a church, taking in street girls and orphans and drunks all because God changed his heart. The Great Physician wants your heart. He wants to take your heart in His hands and cleanse it and make it new. He wants to get your heart ready for the new wine that will be flowing through it. *"All that the Father gives me will come to me, and whoever comes to me I will never drive away"* (John 6:37).

God doesn't have to do anything for us, and yet He does everything. He's under no obligation to us in any way, and yet He extends His grace without measure. Jesus stretched His arms out on the cross and gave Himself up, a perfect sacrifice. He didn't give a little bit of Himself. **Jesus gave everything so that we can have everything God intends, yet so many of us have trouble understanding and living like the Gospel is true.** We constantly want to take the wheel from God's hands and steer the bus ourselves. We hang on to our hearts, refusing to let Him change us. We want to love *our* way. We want to do life *our* way. We constantly resist the heart surgery we so desperately need. Are you ready for heart surgery?

REFLECTION QUESTIONS

1. How ready are you for radical heart surgery at the hands of God?

_____

_____

_____

_____

_____

_____

_____

_____

2. What would radical heart surgery change in your life?

3. Is there anything about God that you are not thrilled about?

WHY LOVE GOD?

"We love because He first loved us."
—1 JOHN 4:19

What makes people love God? We hear all the time that God is good, but what does that mean and is that why we should love Him? Remember the adulterous woman who came to Jesus while He was in the Pharisee's house? She wept at His feet and washed His feet with her tears and her hair. This is what Jesus said in response: *"Therefore, I tell you, her many sins have been forgiven—for she loved much. But he who has been forgiven little loves little"* (Luke 7:47). It's the people who have sinned the most who understand how much they have been forgiven. Perhaps it is easier for them to love Jesus because they *know* how much He has done for them. They understand what sin is and that they're sinners. Those who feel well adjusted and have their lives together and have created their own good self-image often find it hard to understand the magnitude of what Jesus did for us. **People who really see themselves for who they are can more easily see who Jesus is.**

All of us want to be loved, especially by God. We want to know that our Father in heaven always has His heart overflowing with love for us. And that is true and it's a good thing. But there is another side to the relationship. God doesn't want you to just feel warm and fuzzy all the time in His presence. **God wants you to understand what you have been delivered from because, until you see the magnitude of your salvation and realize who you really are without Him, you won't understand His great love and won't be able to properly love Him in return.** There is no condemnation in Christ Jesus (see Rom. 8:1); however, there needs to be awareness on our part. We must not go through life taking our salvation lightly because salvation is a big deal. Ask Jesus!

God wants a reciprocal relationship with you. He gives and you receive, then you give and He receives. He wants your love but He desires genuine love, love that comes from deep in your heart, love that is authentic and real, not something you give lip service to in order to get something from God. We should stand with all of heaven and earth amazed at God's love! *"And this same God who takes care of me will supply all your needs from His glorious riches, which have been given to us in Christ Jesus"* (Phil. 4:19 NLT).

REFLECTION QUESTIONS

1. How do you really see yourself?

_____

_____

_____

_____

_____

2. How do you think God sees you?

_____

3. What does Romans 8:1 means when it says, *"There is now no condemnation for those who are in Christ Jesus"*?

_____

UNENCUMBERED LIVING

"This is what the Lord says: 'Heaven is My throne, and the earth is My footstool. Where is the house you will build for Me? Where will My resting place be?'"
—Isaiah 66:1

A few years ago someone gave me a book by Marguerite Porete, a woman from the fourteenth century in France, titled *The Mirror of Simple Souls*. The book is about divine love and is an exceptionally profound piece of mystical writing. Church authorities considered Porete a threat, and she was eventually burned at the stake for what she wrote and believed. I want to examine several aspects of her writing that are very applicable to what we are studying in regard to building our inner foundation.

First, Porete maintains that once you have fallen completely in love with God, all work ceases—work is done; nothing is work anymore; you are totally and absolutely released from work. What a beautiful truth this is. It is so necessary that you understand this if you are considering the mission field. In missionary work, we get tired all the time. We are weary and we don't know what to do. We often feel terribly encumbered. But God has a remedy for unencumbered living and Porete touched upon it. You see, when you become a Christian and you are joined to Jesus, you become one in spirit and all striving can cease. For many of us it doesn't happen, but it could if we only knew the reality of our relationship with God. When we are joined in spirit with God, His sovereign grace flows through us as pure love. When we fall in love and fall into this place of pure love, there is no striving anymore. Everything flows from a heart of love and is a labor of love. **God's fiery energy enlivens us for whatever He sets in front of us.**

After the crucifixion, Jesus' followers were a frightened, disheartened group of men and women with little support from those around them. They were despised, and many wanted them dead in order to put an end to the notion that the promised Messiah had indeed come. Over the course of forty days, Jesus visited His followers numerous times. He sat and talked with them, walked with them, ate with them, and loved them. As His presence and love overtook them, their hearts began to fall in love with their risen Savior in a new and much deeper way. By the time Pentecost came with the promised Holy Spirit, their hearts were ready to enter into that place of divine love necessary to carry the Gospel to the ends of the earth. God wants His presence and His love to overtake your heart. He wants you to get into that place of unencumbered living that is available to all who love Him because He knows that from this place you can do anything.

REFLECTION QUESTIONS

1. How do you understand the concept of divine love as it impacts unencumbered living?

_____

_____

_____

2. Do we have to go deep into divine love in order to enjoy its benefits?

3. Why do we need divine love to carry the Gospel to the ends of the earth?

HIS WILL

*"For I have come down from heaven not to do My will
but to do the will of Him who sent Me."*
—John 6:38

The second aspect of Marguerite Porete's book that is of importance to our discussion on missions is the surrender of human will to God's will. There is a lot of teaching currently that maintains it is our job in prayer to change God's will. This is in opposition to Scripture. Jesus never taught that we are to seek to impose our will on God. It seems that too often we think we know better than God what needs to be done in a situation. In Mozambique, Heidi and I encounter more impossible situations in one day than many people encounter in a month or a year. Children die of malaria in our arms because there are no resources available to help them. We run out of money for food constantly and have no idea how we are going to feed thousands tomorrow. Children arrive daily at our facilities, sick and traumatized. Trucks break down, people steal from us, the government throws up roadblock after roadblock. There is no possible way for us to take our human will and apply it to these situations and make one whit of difference. We can only submit to His will completely if we are to make it through the day, because He is more than sufficient for all our struggles.

On the very day that we run out of food, a food truck arrives unexpectedly. We have no idea how we are going to feed 400 children with only 25 rolls, and God multiplies the food until every child is fed with enough left over for every child to have two or three rolls, and still the bowls overflow. When a terrible outbreak of cholera hits and hundreds are dying and the doctors say there is no hope, Heidi goes into the makeshift hospital and just sits and holds the sick in the love of Jesus, and the dying stops. Our human will means nothing in the face of the impossible; His will accomplishes the impossible.

Our dependence on God and our love for Him grows every day, making it easier and easier to surrender all to Him. God began building His Church with a handful of people who had no earthly resources and no influence whatsoever. They had no idea how to do what they were called to do outside of submitting to the will of God, and yet in a few hundred years they had taken the Gospel to the world. When you think about it, God hasn't changed His methods much in 2,000 years. He is looking for people to partner with Him who have no resources and no influence and no idea what to do outside of submitting to His will. When He says to throw our nets on the right side of the boat, that's what we do because He is the Lord of the harvest!

REFLECTION QUESTIONS

1. What is it that causes you to think you know better than God what needs to be done in a situation?

2. How hard is it for you to surrender your will to God's will?

3. Are you willing to submit to God's will when it makes absolutely no sense? Most of us like to think we will answer "Yes," but in reality it can be very hard to submit in those kind of circumstances. Why do you think that is?

OUR SIN EVER BEFORE US

"For all have sinned and fall short of the glory of God."
—ROMANS 3:23

A third aspect in Marguerite Porete's book that I want to bring to our attention is one that is difficult for many of us to grasp. Porete maintains that each of us is as bad as the worst sinner imaginable; not one of us is better than anyone else. When we think of someone like Hitler, this concept is one we just can't wrap out minds around. But what Porete is saying is that as soon as we think we're better than someone else, we become encumbered. As soon as we think that we don't need as much grace as someone else, we attach a responsibility to our self that will weigh us down and keep us from the truth of the Gospel.

We are all in desperate need of the grace of Jesus and we should make no mistake about this. We can think we're cleaned up and on the right path with God when in fact we're fast-tracking our way to hell. Think of the apostle Paul. Here was a well-educated man who was zealous in his pursuit to persecute and kill Christians, absolutely convinced that he was on the right path until the grace of God got hold of him. Paul didn't think he was in trouble. To his way of thinking it was the Christians he was pursuing who were the ones in trouble. We mustn't make the mistake of thinking our sins are smaller or less significant than the sins of others lest we consider our self better than others. It's so easy to look at the worst offender and say to yourself, "Whew, I'm glad I'm not that bad." We all do it, either consciously or unconsciously.

As condemning as all of this sounds, it is important to remember that while you are no better than the worst person in the room, nobody is more loved by God than you. That's the dichotomy of the kingdom. We are the worst of sinners and the most beloved of God. That's what we need to understand if we are to go forward in this thing we call the Christian life. Jesus didn't make the ultimate sacrifice because most of us are just little sinners, and He doesn't give us all of His love because our sins are so few. **Jesus knows exactly who we are, and that is precisely why He loves us so much.** Isn't that confusing! Isn't that marvelous! What an amazing life we get to live with Jesus!

REFLECTION QUESTIONS

1. What is your reaction to the idea that you are on par with the worst of sinners?

_____

_____

_____

_____

2. How much of God's grace do you think you need and why?

_____

_____

_____

_____

_____

_____

_____

_____

_____

_____

_____

3. Why do you think Jesus loves you?

_____

_____

_____

_____

_____

_____

_____

_____

_____

_____

SWEET SURRENDER

"Why do you call Me good? No one is good except God alone."
—MARK 10:18 ESV

The fourth and last aspect in Porete's book I want us to reflect on is that of God's absolute goodness and perfection. Let's begin with the premise that when we are in union with God, we agree with Him about everything. That's a picture of a truly unencumbered lifestyle. Because God is perfect, it is impossible for Him to will anything but that which is absolutely the best for you. **He is incapable of being against you and therefore completely trustworthy.** When we learn to live in the reality of God's absolute goodness and perfection, it takes quite a load off our shoulders. It's no longer up to us! Our will can give way completely to His will. When we are so utterly in love with Him, so completely in union with Him—one with Him—we can cease the striving and struggling that encumbers us.

Here in Mozambique we conduct weekly outreaches in the bush. It is a big part of our lifestyle. When we come to a village, there is always so much need. There are blind eyes, deaf ears, crippled limbs, sick and dying people, starving people, abused people, and demonic activity. We see every imaginable permutation of the devil, and if we had our way we would quickly step outside the will of God in trying to deal with these things. But we have learned that God's way and His will are so much better. We typically arrive after dark at the village we are visiting after a long, dusty, bone-rattling ride in the heat. The first thing we do after greeting the people is to set up our beat-up projector and screen and lights so that we can show the Jesus film. They need Jesus first and foremost. Everything else will flow from Him, and so we make the introduction. But it's not the Jesus film that brings them into relationship with Him. It is the person of Jesus Himself manifesting His great love to each person that calls them out of darkness into His marvelous light. When the movie ends, we begin to call for the deaf and blind and lame to come forward and encounter the love of Jesus. Slowly they come, sometimes after an extended period of calling, cautiously curious as to what it means to meet this Jesus they have just learned about. And then He arrives—the first blind eyes are opened and the people begin to feel His presence and His love. As the healings begin to ripple through the people, more blind eyes are healed and deaf ears begin to hear. People are delivered from the demonic. Whole villages come into relationship with Jesus Christ and are forever changed in His manifest presence.

What could be better than this kind of sweet surrender when the goodness and perfection of God is on full display? This is the life we are meant to live, in union with the One who is worthy of it all.

REFLECTION QUESTIONS

1. How well do you know Jesus?

2. If God is completely trustworthy, are you trusting Him completely?

3. When you meet someone in need, what is the first thing you do for them?

CONTEND FOR GOD'S WILL AND DIRECTION

Heidi Baker

"Now on the last day, the great day of the feast, Jesus stood and cried out, saying, "If anyone is thirsty, let him come to Me and drink."
—John 7:37 NASB

SESSION SUMMARY

How hungry and thirsty are you for God's righteousness? Do you long for righteousness on the earth, the kind of righteousness that says no child should die of starvation, no child should be sold as a sex slave, no child should be thrown out in the garbage dump? What will it take for you to live the Beatitudes? Are you ready to become passionate about feeding the hungry with the physical food they need and, more importantly, with the spiritual food they are hungering for? God wants you to be the picture of Jesus Christ in your environment. Are you ready?

Being Jesus to those around you comes with opposition; it comes with persecution. Living the Beatitudes means you will be struck down but not destroyed because God never abandons us. Often you will face a crossroad in ministry. Do you turn to the left or to the right? Only God knows. It is at those crossroad moments you must get on your face and contend for His answer and continue to contend until you feel the spiritual atmosphere begin to shift. Our God is a God who shifts things in order to realign His holy assignments. **We are to be His foot soldiers, fighting for His righteousness for those who cannot fight no matter how the enemy tries to shift us, because the beauty of the Gospel is worthy of our efforts.**

When we stand in faith and walk with Him, He provides because He is the bread of life, the One who multiples food to feed the hungry. When you have His bread in your hands, it's time to take hold of what He has given you and watch it multiply, to take the bread of life, the power of Jesus, the righteousness of God in your hands and go feed as many people as God asks you to feed. He will always be with you in the natural and in the spiritual. He puts His spirit in us so that we can carry the righteousness of Christ and the beauty of Christ into the world. But don't leave home in the morning without His fresh bread in your hands. We can't offer stale bread to the world. It doesn't represent Jesus. He is the fresh bread that comes down from heaven every day. We need to press in close with our hands wide open to receive His precious manna from heaven so that we are fully nourished in order to nourish others. The privilege of carrying the pleasing aroma of His grace to the world is what victorious Christian living looks like. Fill your lamp with oil, your hands with fresh bread, and your heart with the love of Christ and go! The fields are ripe for the harvest.

MAIN CONCEPTS FROM SESSION THIRTEEN

"Now on the last day, the great day of the feast, Jesus stood and cried out, saying, "If anyone is thirsty, let him come to Me and drink."
—John 7:37 NASB

CONTEND FOR GOD'S WILL AND DIRECTION

Heidi Baker

Live the Beatitudes: *"Now when He saw the crowds, He went up on a mountainside and sat down. His disciples came to Him, and He began to teach them, saying: 'Blessed are the poor in spirit, for theirs is the kingdom of heaven. Blessed are those who mourn, for they will be comforted. Blessed are the meek, for they will inherit the earth. Blessed are those who hunger and thirst for righteousness, for they will be filled. Blessed are the merciful, for they will be shown mercy. Blessed are the pure in heart, for they will see God. Blessed are the peacemakers, for they will be called sons of God. Blessed are those who are persecuted because of righteousness, for theirs is the kingdom of heaven. Blessed are you when people insult you, persecute you and falsely say all kinds of evil against you because of Me. Rejoice and be glad, because great is your reward in heaven, for in the same way they persecuted the prophets who were before you.'"* —Matthew 5:1–12

- To be passionate about the Gospel is to hunger for God's righteousness.

- God's righteousness is His perfection in all things—in attitude, behavior, word, and deed.

- Jesus didn't expect us to be able to live the Beatitudes without the power of God working in us.

Contending, Contending, Contending: *"Persecuted, but not abandoned; struck down, but not destroyed."* —2 Corinthians 4:9

- When we are faced with the choice to press forward in the face of great resistance or just quit, it is time to contend for an answer from God.

- All out, passionate worship is a very good way to contend. God will not abandon us in our times of trial.

- Our assignments from God aren't just learning experiences; they are *holy*, just as He is holy.

Surely God Exists: *"Whoever does not love does not know God, because God is love."* —1 John 4:8

- Children who have been orphaned can readily learn what it means to love recklessly and extravagantly, spending lavishly on sacrifice, if they themselves have been treated like prodigals.

- Instead of chastising us when we squander what He gives us, God always welcomes us back into His embrace when we come to Him. He wants us to do the same for others.

Multiplication: *"'We have here only five loaves of bread and two fish,' they answered. 'Bring them here to Me,' He said. And He directed the people to sit down on the grass. Taking the five loaves and the two fish and looking up to heaven, He gave thanks and broke the loaves. Then He gave them to the disciples, and the disciples gave them to the people. They all ate and were satisfied, and the disciples picked up twelve basketfuls of broken pieces that were left over. The number of those who ate was about five thousand men, besides women and children."* —Matthew 14:17–21

- God is performing miracles of multiplication today just as He has done throughout history.

- Multiplication miracles are hard to believe unless you see them with your own eyes because we are slow to understand and embrace the reality of the supernatural.

Fresh Bread: *"Then the Lord said to Moses, 'I will rain down bread from heaven for you. The people are to go out each day and gather enough for that day.'"* —Exodus 16:4

- People have a tendency to quickly forget what God has done for them.

- No matter how great a miracle He gives us, we are quick to find something that is not to our liking.

- God desires that we come close to Him every day in order to carry His supernatural presence to those who are in need of Him. The longer we stay away from Him, the less of His presence we have.

- His presence is the "fresh bread" we have to sustain us and to give away.

Session Thirteen Devotions

LIVE THE BEATITUDES

The beatitudes are a powerful picture of Jesus' life. If we are to be imitators of Christ, each one of us needs a picture of the Lord Jesus to carry in our hearts. We need to know Jesus so intimately so that we understand what He looks like, how He "walks," how He talks, what is in His heart. We must know Jesus intimately if we are to represent Him well on the earth so that when people see us, they see Jesus. We must learn to live the Beatitudes.

> *Now when He saw the crowds, He went up on a mountainside and sat down. His disciples came to Him, and He began to teach them, saying: "Blessed are the poor in spirit, for their's is the kingdom of heaven. Blessed are those who mourn, for they will be comforted. Blessed are the meek, for they will inherit the earth. Blessed are those who hunger and thirst for righteousness, for they will be filled. Blessed are the merciful, for they will be shown mercy. Blessed are the pure in heart, for they will see God. Blessed are the peacemakers, for they will be called sons of God. Blessed are those who are persecuted because of righteousness, for theirs is the kingdom of heaven. Blessed are you when people insult you, persecute you and falsely say all kinds of evil against you because of Me. Rejoice and be glad, because great is your reward in heaven, for in the same way they persecuted the prophets who were before you"* (Matthew 5:1–12).

If we do not live the Beatitudes, how will the mourning be comforted? How will the hungry be fed? No child should die of starvation in a world where there is obesity. No child should suffer when we have the technology and the ability to feed them, when hundreds of tons of food are dumped in the oceans to keep prices high. This is not acceptable and we should refuse to accept it. At times Iris has fed 100,000 people a day for four and five months in a row. At a minimum 22,000 people a day are fed through Iris. Obviously we're very passionate about feeding people physical food, but we are equally passionate that all receive spiritual food. We not only want to see everyone receive spiritual food, we want to see this spiritual food multiply. We long for righteousness on the earth, the kind of righteousness that says no child should die of starvation, no child should be sold as a sex slave, no child should be thrown out in the garbage dump. How hungry and thirsty are you for God's righteousness? What will it take for you to begin to live the Beatitudes?

REFLECTION QUESTIONS

1. Heidi ends this devotion with two questions. How would you answer them?

_____

_____

_____

_____

_____
_____
_____
_____
_____
_____
_____
_____
_____
_____

2. What would it look like for you to be a picture of Jesus in your current environment?

_____
_____
_____
_____
_____
_____
_____
_____
_____
_____
_____
_____
_____
_____
_____

REFLECTION

Jesus gave His Sermon on the Mount as a standard for all Christians, knowing that we could not possibly live these things out without God's power. That doesn't mean that we can't live the Beatitudes—it means that with God these things are possible as both a present reality and a future hope. If you are overwhelmed by the Beatitudes, don't try and accomplish all of them. Start with one because one is better than none. Trust God to be strong where you are weak.

CONTENDING, CONTENDING, CONTENDING!

"Persecuted, but not abandoned; struck down, but not destroyed."
—2 Corinthians 4:9

So many times Iris Global has faced a crossroad, a point in the road where we wonder if God is going to continue the ministry or just shut it down. One of our crossroad times occurred during the high holiday of another religious faith. We were in the middle of a Harvest School, and suddenly the government revoked the visas of a hundred or so of our students along with the visas of many of our workers. It was a devastating blow in the natural. We began to question God as to whether we were to press on or close many of our operations. In the midst of our own hunger for righteousness in Mozambique—the place we have invested all of our heart for so many years—we knew we had to be able to lay it down if that was God's will. We just needed to hear from Him. God does things His own way and we need to stick with His plan.

When Rolland was three years old, he and his family barely escaped from China. They were forced to abandon their mission, in a boat, with machine guns firing at their backs. But funny thing was, when all the missionaries left China, the Church grew faster than it had ever grown in the history of the world. The greatest church growth came during persecution. As we cried out to God day and night about our visa situation in Mozambique, I recalled what God had done in China when He sent the missionaries out, and I knew in my heart that if He sent us out of Mozambique, we would trust Him for the outcome. We were ready to stay or ready to go. We just needed a sign from God, so we got on our faces and began to worship. Day and night we worshiped the Lord in the huts and in the villages, and then things began to shift. We could literally feel the shift in our spirits.

As things shifted, God reminded me that we aren't on an assignment here at Iris from Him just to learn. We are on a *holy* assignment from Him. There is a holy purpose in everything He does. **We may get confused, but God is never confused**. He knows we will be shaken, struck down, but not destroyed because we always carry around in our bodies the death of Jesus, so that the life of Jesus may also be revealed in our bodies (see 2 Cor. 4:9-10). When trouble comes, we must contend, contend again, and then contend some more because God promises not to abandon us.

REFLECTION QUESTIONS

1. What crossroad times have you faced in your life and how did you contend?

_____

_____

_____

_____

2. Would you be willing to give up something you've invested all of your heart in and years of your life if God told you it was time to walk away, or would you fight on?

3. Can you recall an instance in your life when God has abandoned you? If so, reflect on who abandoned whom.

SURELY GOD EXISTS

"Whoever does not love does not know God, because God is love."
—1 John 4:8

One day in the midst of the visa struggle, I was out and about in Mozambique when I came across one of our prodigal sons who had run away yet again. We found him on the streets begging when he was young and brought him home with us, but he just couldn't follow the rules. He would run away and come back, then run away again, then come back again. It became a very trying and difficult situation. This particular day I found him sleeping in the latrines. He was curled up in a ball sleeping in a latrine. My heart broke. "God," I cried out, "surely we exist for this one! Surely we exist for children such as these!" As I knelt beside him, he said, "Mom, there's no food in my house. I'm really, really hungry." Long story short, it didn't take much for him to jump in the back of my truck and head home with me. When we got back to our base and the kids saw this precious one had come home, they ran out shouting and screaming for joy, welcoming him back! They started laughing and dancing, and we celebrated by buying bananas for everyone. We had a party because our prodigal son came home.

For me this was one of the signs from God that we were to continue in Mozambique. God exists so that we can exist for every child who has to sleep in a latrine. Most of the time we have to fight to exist, but as long as it is God's will, we fight. We fight for His righteousness on the earth, fight for children to be safe, fight for their education, fight so that the Gospel can go forth and lives can be transformed. We fight to push back on corruption that takes the necessities of life out of the hands of the poor to line the pockets of the rich. We fight for basic electricity, roads to drive on, wells for water. We fight for a lot of things here every day in Mozambique, but most of all we contend for the beauty of the Gospel. It's a battle that we can't win, but He can win. We are His foot soldiers. We dig our heels in, learning to love, believing that there is always enough and that the hungry will be fed as long as we are compelled by His love.

REFLECTION QUESTIONS

1. Why were the children on the Iris base so excited to see one child return home?

------

2. A prodigal is someone who squanders resources recklessly. What resources did the prodigal son in Heidi's story squander?

3. Do we need to become better prodigals before we can properly welcome home the prodigals?

4. How do we learn to love recklessly and extravagantly, lavishly spending on sacrifice?

MULTIPLICATION

"'We have here only five loaves of bread and two fish,' they answered. 'Bring them here to Me,' He said. And He directed the people to sit down on the grass. Taking the five loaves and the two fish and looking up to heaven, He gave thanks and broke the loaves. Then He gave them to the disciples, and the disciples gave them to the people. They all ate and were satisfied, and the disciples picked up twelve basketfuls of broken pieces that were left over. The number of those who ate was about five thousand men, besides women and children."
—MATTHEW 14:17–21

God is truly the God of multiplication, but until you've seen it and experienced it, it can be very hard to believe. We've seen a lot of multiplication in Mozambique, but most of the students, no matter how much they've studied the supernatural, can't wrap their minds around it. There is one multiplication story in particular that stands out in my mind. It happened in Maputo during the floods. Thousands were displaced, living in refugee camps, and we were busy trying to care for them. There was one camp called "Camp 2000" because there were literally 2,000 men living there, not counting their wives and the children who typically number between five and seven children per family. Suffice to say, there were a lot of people living in Camp 2000.

Everything around the refuge camps was destroyed. The roads were gone. There was nothing.

I remember the Lord speaking very clearly to me, telling me that we were to feed 5,000 people a day. At the time that was such an impossibility that it was humorous to even think about it, but that's what God said. And so I said, "Yes, Lord. We'll do it," having no idea how. At the time we had somewhere between $200-300 in our Iris account. We might as well of had two or three cents for all the good our pittance was in terms of feeding 5,000 people. Then I heard the Lord say, "Call the government and tell them you're going to feed 5,000 people a day," so I called them and told them and they were grateful. Then I had to call Rolland and our staff and tell them what I had just done. We didn't even have the money to feed ourselves, and now I had committed to feed 5,000. We went to bed that night with not a clue about what to do the next day, and that's when God showed up. A church in the UK wired us their entire savings for the building program, 30,000 British pounds, which at the time was close to 60,000 USD! The church didn't know anything about our promise. It was a crazy miracle.

We went out and bought all the food we could find in the city. Now, for those of you who have spent time in Maputo, you know about the bread. There's a certain kind of bread in Maputo that's delicious. The loaves have a special flavor from being cooked in a certain type of oven. We bought every loaf we could find in the city, which totaled about 1,000 loaves, then we counted them because when you are feeding lots of people you need to know how much food you have if you are to make any sort of a fair and even distribution.

But the best was yet to come. We took our loaves back to Camp 2000 and got things set up for distribution by our students. Mind you, these students were from a school of *supernatural* ministry. So there we were, with 1,000 loaves for 2,000 men plus their women and children. You can do the math—a lot of people, not enough bread. I knew what God was going to do, but the students just couldn't understand. When I told them to feed the people and not to break the loaves up into little tiny pieces, they thought I was nuts. The looks on their faces said it all. "They're going to kill us," they said. "There's going to be a riot and they are going to kill us!" I said, "Listen sweethearts, this happens all the time. All you need to do is...well first, let's pray." So we lined up all the bags of bread, laid our hands on them and we prayed, then I went off to be with the chiefs and government officials in order to honor them. When I returned a few hours later our Harvest School students were literally jumping around and leaping and praising God with tears streaming down their faces. They had approximately the same number of bags full of bread as when they started and everyone had been fed. Not only had everyone been fed, but everyone had been given a whole loaf! We took the overflow bags to the chief. It was glorious.

Jesus is the bread of life, and when you have His bread in your hands it's time to take hold of what He has given you and see it multiply. You take the bread of life, the power of Jesus, the righteousness of Jesus in your hands and you go and feed any number of people God asks you to feed because He is a living God. He won't just be with you in the natural. He'll be with you in the spiritual. There is extraordinary poverty on the earth and you have the bread of life in your hands. You have the righteousness of Christ, the beauty of Christ and it's time for you to start lifting up your little offering to the One who is worthy and ask Him to multiply you for the multitudes. It's time to be multiplied!

REFLECTION QUESTIONS

1. Do you believe this story of multiplication, and why or why not?

2. We speak metaphorically of Jesus, the bread of life, being in our hands. What does that mean?

_____

_____

_____

_____

_____

_____

_____

_____

_____

_____

_____

_____

_____

_____

_____

_____

3. Because multiplication is happening today, just as it did in Jesus' time, does that make it any easier for you to accept the reality that other types of miracles are also happening today?

_____

_____

_____

_____

_____

_____

_____

_____

_____

_____

_____

_____

_____

_____

FRESH BREAD

"Then the Lord said to Moses, 'I will rain down bread from heaven for you.
The people are to go out each day and gather enough for that day.'"
—Exodus 16:4

If you go to the Book of Exodus, chapter 16, and start reading, you'll find that it wasn't that long after God led the Israelites out of captivity that they began to grumble against Him. In fact, the Scriptures say they were just two months out of captivity when the whole community grumbled against Moses and Aaron. *"If only we had died by the Lord's hand in Egypt!"* they cried. *"There we sat around pots of meat and ate all the food we wanted, but you have brought us out into this desert to starve this entire assembly to death"* (Exod. 16:3). God responded to the hunger of His people by raining down fresh bread and meat from heaven every day! The people of Israel called the bread "manna," and it sustained them for forty years until they reached the Promised Land.

God's presence is like manna, fresh bread for those who are hungry. We must pray for the bread of life, the presence of God, every day. We need fresh bread for ourselves and fresh bread to give away. We can't live on stale bread and we certainly don't want to give away stale bread. Here in Mozambique, in the dirt and the heat, bread doesn't stay fresh for long. If we have it and don't eat it or give it away, it will spoil very quickly, in a day. Spoiled bread is a terrible waste when people are starving. That same principle applies in a spiritual sense. When people are starved for the presence of God, for His fresh bread, it is our responsibility to provide them with the best manna possible, the freshest bread possible. How do you do that? You do that by feeding on fresh bread yourself.

When you fly in an airplane, the flight attendant always gives the required safety talk at the beginning of the flight. When he or she gets to the part about the oxygen mask, you are instructed to put the mask on yourself first and then help someone else, because if you don't have adequate oxygen you'll be of no use to anyone. Likewise, when we don't stay close to the freshness of God's presence, it's impossible to give it away. We must press in close and then closer still until His sweet aroma permeates every fiber of our being, until we smell like Him. This is what it means to live victoriously in Christ, to be given the privilege of carrying the pleasing aroma of His grace to the world. What a beautiful thing to be the sweet aroma of God, with hands full of His fresh bread to give to the hungry!

REFLECTION QUESTIONS

1. Have you ever been set free from bondage of some sort only to find yourself dissatisfied because life still wasn't as good as you thought it should be? How did God respond to your dissatisfaction?

2. How do you think we manage to keep our supply of "fresh bread" in the midst of the chaos and challenges of Mozambique?

3. How do you feel about the idea of "smelling like God," and what does that really mean?

LAY DOWN YOUR LIFE

Rolland Baker

*"This is how we know what love is: Jesus Christ laid down his life
for us. And we ought to lay down our lives for our brothers."*
—1 John 3:16

SESSION SUMMARY

Laying down your life in the mission field is a glorious goal for those called by God. This kind of lifestyle will take you to a place where faith is absolutely necessary; therefore, it is vitally important that you understand the nature of faith. What is faith, where does it come from, and why do we need it? Our faith in God is based on complete trust and confidence in Him—on a strong belief in Him based on our spiritual understanding rather than proof. To have this kind of faith, we need to be in an intimate relationship with God so that His Spirit can constantly put His presence and His truths in our heart.

Many today are confused about the nature of faith and about who God is. New Age teaching, characterized by alternative approaches to traditional Western culture, operates with an occult-based spirituality that is in direct opposition to the Scriptures and to Jesus Christ. When we are living outside of a close and intimate relationship with God, it is easy to be deceived by false teaching. When we have the fresh, authentic presence of God in our lives every day, it is easier to spot the devil and His imposters.

Missions will bring you in contact with the poor in spirit, those with a pure heart who hunger for God. In that place of desperation for Him that takes precedence over everything else, you will find people who are joyful because, unencumbered by the things of the world, they are able to come into His presence in the power of His Spirit. With pure, happy, humble hearts, they live life dependent on God's mercy as they earnestly seek Him. Theirs is truly the kingdom of heaven!

Life in the kingdom of God requires that we learn to operate within the multiple perspectives of Scripture. This holy multiplicity is God's design, and we must embrace it rather than choosing what we like best and discarding the rest. **God gives us both sides of an issue for a reason, and even when we don't understand His reasoning we need to understand that His sovereignty deserves our respect.** When we are weak, He is strong. When we are poor, He is rich. **God will put us in a place of great need and then come and meet our needs in the most spectacular ways to display His glory.** Missions is best done from a place of need where God has room to do His will.

MAIN CONCEPTS FROM SESSION FOURTEEN

"This is how we know what love is: Jesus Christ laid down His life
for us. And we ought to lay down our lives for our brothers."
—1 JOHN 3:16

LAY DOWN YOUR LIFE

Rolland Baker

Faith and the Power of God: *"For in the gospel the righteousness of God is revealed, a righteousness that is by faith from first to last, just as it is written: 'The righteous will live by faith.'"* —Romans 1:17

- Our faith in God is based on complete trust and confidence in Him; on a strong belief in Him based on our spiritual understanding rather than proof.

- We must be in an intimate relationship with God in order to have faith in Him.

- We need to understand what faith is not lest we be deceived by New Age practices that are not of God.

God Doesn't Need Our Help: *"In the last days, God says, I will pour out My Spirit on all people. Your sons and daughters will prophesy, your young men will see visions, your old men will dream dreams."* —Acts 2:17

- God doesn't need us to be His public relations agents on the earth.

- Although God doesn't need us, He *wants us* close to Him.

- God will display Himself through all flesh, pouring His Spirit on all flesh in the last days, not because of anything we do, but because He is the sovereign God of all.

Starving for God: *"Blessed are the poor in Spirit, for theirs is the kingdom of heaven."* —Matthew 5:3

- The human heart's hunger for God takes precedence over everything else, even over physical hunger.

- It is easier to come into relationship with God (to "see" God) when our hearts are pure. Those who are "poor in spirit" are the pure in heart.

- The pure in heart are joyful because they are able to come into His presence in the power of His Spirit.

- The pure in heart are happy, humble, repentant, dependent on the mercy of God and constantly earnestly seeking God.

Strategy for Ministry: *"And my God will meet all your needs according to His glorious riches in Christ Jesus."* —Philippians 4:19

- When we are in times of greatest need, God will come and meet our needs in the most spectacular ways just to remind us that He is our provider.

- It is when we have nothing that we are well positioned to receive from God.

- When missions is done from a place of need, God has room to do His will.

Romans 9: *"'I will have mercy on whom I have mercy, and I will have compassion on whom I have compassion.' It does not, therefore, depend on man's desire or effort, but on God's mercy."* —Romans 9:15-16

- The kingdom of God operates with a holy tension.

- The nature of Scripture is that it is contradictory; it will say one thing, then turn around and say the opposite.

- We must be careful not to pick sides when confronted with the holy tension of Scripture. God gives us both viewpoints for a reason. It is up to us to look for understanding in all of Scripture.

Session Fourteen Devotions

FAITH AND THE POWER OF GOD

"For in the gospel the righteousness of God is revealed, a righteousness that is by faith from first to last, just as it is written: 'The righteous will live by faith.'"
—Romans 1:17

People often ask me what my definition of faith is. I see a lot of people treating faith like some sort of power or force that's given to us or something we get from somewhere that gives us the ability to make God do things, as if we are in control and can make things happen according to our will. This is not the faith of the Bible. This is a description of the New Age version of faith. Sadly, the New Age version of faith is what a lot of people want, even in the Church. They want to know how to take God's power and use it for their purposes. Then there are those who think that the words of the Bible have power and that all we have to do is quote Scripture to wield power. In the midst of the confusion about faith, the bottom line is people are interested in the power of God, sometimes for good and godly reasons and sometimes not.

It's important to understand that faith isn't an inanimate, impersonal force that we just throw around. **Faith is knowing God well enough to know what *He* wants to do in a given situation.** One aspect of faith is the understanding that God isn't going to do anything that goes against His nature, and so we shouldn't be asking Him to. We can pray all day, asking God to do this and that, but God will do what He wants to do, period. He is not a force that anyone or anything can order around. Often, when prayers aren't answered people will tell you that you just need more faith, but what is faith?

If you look up the definition of faith you'll find this: "Complete trust or confidence in someone or something; a strong belief in God or in the doctrines of a religion, based on spiritual apprehension rather than proof," *apprehension* being "understanding" in this instance. So let's take that definition and put it in the context of a relationship with God. Our faith in God is based on complete trust and confidence in Him, on a strong belief in Him based on our spiritual understanding rather than proof. In other words, we must be in an intimate relationship with God to have actually faith in Him. Intimacy implies that we are very close to someone, very familiar with them. Intimate relationships happen between parents and children who are close because of their love for one another. Most children quickly come to know what their parents like and don't like. Children know what they can ask for and when not to ask because they know their parents intimately. That's the kind of relationship God wants with us. He wants us, His beloved sons and daughters, to know Him so intimately that we know His heart. He wants us close all the time, intimate all the time, so that our faith can be fresh and real and available when we need it, because He knows we're going to need it! Whether you're in the mission field abroad or the mission field of your office, you're going to need an intimate relationship with God and the faith that comes from knowing Him.

REFLECTION QUESTIONS

1. Describe the nature of faith as you understand it.

2. What does Rolland mean when he refers to the "New Age version of faith"? What is New Age?

3. What does Scripture mean when it says the righteous will live by faith?

GOD DOESN'T NEED OUR HELP

"In the last days, God says, I will pour out My Spirit on all people. Your sons and daughters will prophesy, your young men will see visions, your old men will dream dreams."
—Acts 2:17

I think we have established by now that God likes relationship, but there are certain aspects of that relationship that we need to understand. A lot of people think it is our job to make God look good, that we are supposed to be His public relations agents on the earth. That's not true. God doesn't need us to make Him look good. He is quite capable of doing that Himself. **It's not that God needs us; He *wants* us. He prefers to do things with us and through us rather than just doing everything Himself.** He puts His Spirit in us, therefore He lives in us. We are His people. We are how God chooses to express Himself, to display Himself. He has chosen us to partner with Him because He likes it that way. God likes relationship, and He wants a relationship with *everyone*. Notice I emphasized *everyone* because God is no respecter of persons. He will often bypass the most "qualified" and use the most unlikely person to display His glory.

My friend Bob was one of those "unlikelies." Bob was a big bear of a guy who immigrated to the US from Europe. He was rough and tough and uneducated. Bob joined the Navy and became a frogman (similar to a Navy Seal). He was a really tough guy and very far away from God. One day the Holy Spirit fell on him, knocked him to the ground, and left him there, blind for three days. When Bob got up off that floor he was a prophet. From that day onward, Bob led the most amazing and miraculous life. He and I became good friends. He was so prophetic that I rarely talked to him because he already knew what was on my mind.

Bob decided to open a weightlifting gym as a way to minister to troubled youth. The gym quickly became a ministry center. Jesus was always very present in that place. Bob was an incredible weightlifter, and eventually he became the coach of the world champion power lifting team. He knew all the famous body builders. He had this incredible prophetic gift and the strength of Sampson. I couldn't wait to get down to the gym every day just to see what God was going to do. Miracle after miracle flowed from Bob.

One of my favorite Bob stories is the waterfall story. As Bob tells it, one night he went to bed only to be awakened in the middle of the night to the sound of rushing water. It sounded like water pouring over rocks. He got out of bed and went to see what was going on. As he looked down the stairs into the living room he saw this huge waterfall pouring down from the top of the stairs into the living room. The furniture was floating around and being swept outside and into the swimming pool. Bob watched this for about half an hour thinking it was a vision. This is a man who was very used to hearing from God, but at that moment he heard nothing. Finally he decided to go back to bed, figuring God would explain things in the morning. When Bob got up the next morning he discovered what he saw the night before was no vision. His living room was a sopping wet mess and the furniture was in the swimming pool. He didn't know what to make of it. God was silent for three days and then He spoke. "Bob," He said, "this is how

I'm going to pour out My Spirit on all flesh in the last days. I know how to look after My own reputation. I know how to glorify Myself. I know how to bring My Son back. I know how to finish history in this world, and I don't need any help from you."

What's the point? The point is simple—God doesn't need our help; He just wants it. He wants us close, He wants us in relationship. He loves us and wants us to love Him in return. It is you God wants. It is you He has chosen to display Himself through. Are you willing?

REFLECTION QUESTIONS

1. What is Rolland saying when he says that God doesn't need our help?

2. If God doesn't need our help, why does He want to partner with us?

3. How is God no respecter of persons? What does that mean?

STARVING FOR GOD

"Blessed are the poor in Spirit, for theirs is the kingdom of heaven."
—Matthew 5:3

In 2000, Mozambique experienced one of the worst natural disasters in the history of the world. Three cyclones came together causing torrential rain for forty days and forty nights. A third of the villages were washed out to sea. You couldn't tell where the ground ended and the ocean began. People were having babies in trees. A third of the children couldn't find their parents; they just vanished without a trace. Dead cows and bodies were floating everywhere. We would go to refugee camps in the pouring rain with trucks of bread and people would scream, "We don't want your bread. Take it home. We want God!" We started taking boxes of tracts and throwing them up in the wind so that they would blow all over the place and people could pick them up. People nearly tore my clothes off trying to get tracts. They were demanding pastors and churches, *now*; "We need God now!" they cried. When we talked to the President's Chief of Staff, he said Mozambique didn't need all the humanitarian aid organizations; they needed love—they needed God. A cry went out to God from all over the country like we've never seen or heard, and then God began raising people from the dead. Signs and wonders exploded across the country. The people's hunger brought the presence of God. We never could have planned any of it. It was all God.

Mozambique experienced five hundred years of colonialism and slavery under European power. Then came revolution, communism, and atheism, all of which resulted in complete destruction of the economy and the country's infrastructure. All of this was followed by the flood of 2000. Mozambique was brought to its knees and began to cry out for God. Can you imagine what it is like to be literally starving to death and wanting God more than food? There is a hunger in the human heart that only God can satisfy. We are the ones with hands full of fresh bread, carriers of His presence. **God wants the fire of His love to burn in our hearts until we can do nothing but love Him, nothing but give Him everything, nothing but die so that others might live.**

Mozambique is still full of people starving for God. They come with nothing, walking for days in the heat and the dirt with only the clothes on their backs. They have nothing to offer Him but themselves and that is all God wants. They sit and listen to Bible teaching for hours and then ask for more. They worship with utter abandon all day, and then ask to worship into the night. Young and old alike are desperate for Him. Children give themselves over to worship, tears streaming down their faces as He draws close. Oh, that all people everywhere could know such hunger for God!

REFLECTION QUESTIONS

1. Try and list at least four characteristics of those who are "poor in spirit."

2. What is another term for poor in spirit?

3. What does it mean to "see God"?

STRATEGY FOR MINISTRY

"And my God will meet all your needs according to His glorious riches in Christ Jesus."
—Philippians 4:19

In all the years we've been in ministry, even long before Iris, we have always had a radical approach to missions. We've never turned to the left or to the right to get money from anyone. We've never written a newsletter or had a conference for that reason. We're not trying to get anything out of anybody. And we don't try to talk people into joining Iris either. In the early days, when we were ministering in Asia, we had teams that we would take out for six months at a time. We would tell people, "Look, you really don't want to do this. We are going to China and don't know if we're coming back alive." We were radical for God. We would spend every last dime we had on a one-way ticket, not knowing what we would do when we arrived, where we would sleep, how we would eat. We would sit on the curb at the airport and just pray and God would show up.

In those days we did dance drama—theater in the streets. We were not pastors or experienced speakers. We had a professional speaker on our team to help us. But our team of dancers, actors, and acrobats got a lot of attention. Once in an airport terminal we didn't know what we were going to do next, so one of our guys started doing some entertaining on a skateboard. As it happened there was a man there, a devout Christian, who worked for a hotel chain. When he found out that we did Christian street drama, he summoned some vans and began arranging housing and ministry for us all over the city. Within an hour we had a full preaching schedule, all the food we needed, and places to stay. This same sort of thing happened everywhere we went.

On one particular trip in Indonesia, we found ourselves in an old, rickety, un-air-conditioned bus, bouncing over beat-up roads for hours in the heat and the dust. It was brutal even for us. The trip took almost twenty-four hours. At one point we had to stop in a big, dirty industrial city and wait nine hours in a hole-in-the-wall station for our next bus. We were bruised and exhausted. We were going to sit in steamy, miserable heat in the dirt all night. The soot was so thick you could draw all over your face. There was a pit latrine in the corner with broken glass windows. You would go in there and little Indonesian boys would press their noses up against the broken glass to watch you. There was nothing to eat or drink, but we had no money so it didn't matter.

My younger sister was with us, and at one point she just blurted out, "Oh, God, we want ice cream!" Before we left Bali we had taken in a poor older gentleman, a destitute old farmer. He had no money for a ticket, so we bought him one and he came along with our team. When my sister blurted out to God that we could use some ice cream, this dear man sprang to life. He had once been a successful businessman and had a friend in the town we were in who owned an ice cream factory. Long story short, he called his friend who came and picked us up, took us to his mansion where his servants fed us all kinds of ice cream—all we could eat—while we swam in his pool. And as if that wasn't enough, we were then treated to an amazing Indonesian feast. God just wanted to make sure we understood that He provides!

God took care of us in those days, and we learned to trust Him for every little tiny thing. He engineered everything and that is the way it has been ever since. **When people ask me my strategy for ministry, I tell them that God will provide.**

REFLECTION QUESTIONS

1. How does God provide *"according to His glorious riches in Christ Jesus"*?

_____

_____

_____

_____

_____

_____

_____

2. What would it take for you to have the kind of faith to buy a one-way ticket to a remote place in need of the Gospel, not knowing anyone, not having any resources?

_____

_____

_____

_____

_____

_____

_____

_____

3. What is it that compels Rolland and Heidi to such a radical life?

_____

_____

_____

_____

_____

_____

_____

_____

ROMANS 9

"'I will have mercy on whom I have mercy, and I will have compassion on whom I have compassion.' It does not, therefore, depend on man's desire or effort, but on God's mercy."
—ROMANS 9:15-16

If something is in the Bible, it's there for a reason. God put it there because we need it, and if we need something from God we ought to accept it. Many have a hard time accepting chapter 9 in the Book of Romans. Preachers don't preach on it, commentaries don't comment on it. Everyone likes to avoid Romans 9 because they can't figure out how to make sense of it. Many years ago I attended Calvary Chapel with Pastor Chuck Smith. Chuck was an amazing teacher. He would teach going straight through the Bible. I loved his teachings. They were recorded on cassette tapes and I treasured them. The first time I went through the Bible with Chuck at Calvary Chapel, I couldn't wait for him to teach on Romans 9. I wanted to hear what this man of God had to say about this difficult chapter in the Bible. I rushed to the bookstore to buy his tape on Romans 9 and drove home quickly to listen to it. Chuck skipped chapter 9. It was the only chapter in the Bible he skipped, as if it didn't exist.

If we are going to understand the Bible, we need to understand that God's perfections are often expressed in dichotomies. These multiple perspectives make sense in His kingdom. If you hear preaching that doesn't acknowledge the dichotomies inherent in Scripture, don't accept it. Romans 9, as hard as it is to grasp, comes out and states plainly that it's not up to us who runs the world because God is sovereign. Period. That's what it says. That's what God wants us to understand in Romans 9. Yes, there are other things to be learned in Romans 9, but in the end it is about the sovereignty of God. The promises Jesus purchased on the cross with His blood will be carried to completion by God's sovereign power. God is in charge and we are not and that's a good thing.

How terrible it would be if we were not able to experience the freedom of God's love, if we were forced to be machines. And it would be equally terrible if God were not in control. He orchestrates all things according to His perfect will. As the Holy Spirit controls us and changes our hearts to conform with His heart, we experience sovereignty as desire to obey Him. We must be careful not to pick sides when confronted with the dichotomy of the Scriptures. We may prefer one side over another, but God didn't give us just one side. Many people embrace the teaching that we have a good heavenly Father who would never cause His children to suffer while rejecting parts of the Bible that clearly say we will suffer for our faith, such as First Peter 4:19: *"Those who suffer according to God's will should commit themselves to their faithful Creator and continue to do good."* If we throw away our faith in the midst of trials and temptations, we miss the opportunity to glorify God.

PRAYER

"Lord, I pray that You will cement this understanding of First Peter 4:19 in everyone's heart and mind. We absolutely set our feet on Your Word. We plant ourselves on You, the Rock of

salvation. We hide ourselves in You, depending on You utterly for everything, trusting not in our own abilities and our reason. No matter what happens, we trust You with all our hearts. For this reason, we can love You and enjoy You and enjoy thinking about You seriously just as much as we do move joyfully. We give You everything because Your salivation is so good. I pray people will come to understand more than ever the content of Your salvation, what it means to be saved, what it means to fully trust, what it means to be for You, what it means to have a perfect future, an absolute carefree existence, the capacity to understand with all the saints the height and breadth and length and depth of the love of God. Amen."

Session Fifteen

LOVERS OF JESUS

Rolland Baker

"In the beginning was the Word, and the Word was with God, and the Word was God. …And the Word became flesh and dwelt among us, and we have seen His glory, glory as of the only Son from the Father, full of grace and truth."
—John 1:1,14 ESV

SESSION SUMMARY

God is inviting us to fall in love with Him, to participate in a divine romance that takes us beyond the physical aspects of love with a vision that goes deep inside the heart, showing us what will be possible in heaven. There is something very romantic about God that exceeds any human experience. When we truly "fall in love with God," bells go off in our head and our heart and suddenly we are in love with God and it's the most powerful love in the universe. Nothing can quench it. Nothing can take God's love away from you. This is a love so pure and so strong that you'll die for it. We were created to love God. We were made for *Him*. God wants to be loved. He's romantic and He wants a partner. He wants a bride. He wants a people, children, companionship, and friendship. He didn't just create us to bless us and have us do what He says. Our primary job as Christians and missionaries is to love God. That's what God desires. Love is what Jesus gave God first and foremost. Everything Jesus did flowed from His love relationship with His Father. If you take even the most cursory glance at the teachings of Jesus, you will very quickly come to the aspect of loving God. That's where the Christian life is intended to begin. **Before we came into this world, each one of us began in the heart of God. He is our heart's true home.**

A supernatural life of miracles should be normal for Christians, but sadly it isn't. Most of the Christian world doesn't believe in miracles. They send their missionaries to poor pagan countries and find out the devil is the only one doing things, or so they say. Why would anyone be willing to give their life for a god who doesn't do anything? How can you obey a god who doesn't speak? The miraculous is an integral part of a life lived in Jesus. We must learn to value His power, not for our own sakes, as a way to gain notice, but because it demonstrates His great love. We are different from all other religions because of God's power. Desperate people aren't interested in good preaching. They desperately need the power of God working through love in faith—this is what we must carry to the lost and broken. When Jesus comes to town, the needy will walk hundreds of miles barefoot, without food, wading through waist-deep mud just to be in His presence because His presence has all that they need.

This world needs a powerful God and we have one! He is our all-powerful King Jesus. Hallelujah! Let us surrender every part of us for every part of Him with a willingness to step out of a natural lifestyle and into His supernatural lifestyle of love. He is waiting!

MAIN CONCEPTS FROM SESSION FIFTEEN

"In the beginning was the Word, and the Word was with God, and the Word was God. …And the Word became flesh and dwelt among us, and we have seen His glory, glory as of the only Son from the Father, full of grace and truth."
—John 1:1,14 ESV

LOVERS OF JESUS

Rolland Baker

Falling in Love: *"Many waters cannot quench love; nor will rivers overflow it; if a man were to give all the riches of his house for love, it would be utterly despised."* —Song of Solomon 8:7 NASB

- Falling in love with God is about participating in a divine romance.

- In Scripture, God aims to give us a picture of what divine romance is by using human romance as an example in Song of Solomon.

- Many people get confused by Scripture about divine romance because of the physical/sexual aspect of human romance.

- Divine romance with God is not about physical attraction. It is about a spiritual relationship.

- In divine romance, God takes us beyond the physical aspects of love with a vision that goes deep inside the heart, showing us what is possible in heaven.

Made for God: *"I have found David the son of Jesse, a man after My heart, who will do all My will."* —Acts 13:22 NASB

- God created us for Himself because He wants to be loved; He wants a bride, a people, children, companionship, and friendship.

- We are uniquely designed by God to love Him.

- Our primary job as missionaries and believers is to love God.

- Jesus is our example of what it means to love God.

- God wants us to live a life that is "heart based" not "work based."

Miracles: *"Every good and perfect gift is from above, coming down from the Father of the heavenly lights, who does not change like shifting shadows."* —James 1:17

- We value the miraculous power of God because it demonstrates His love.

- The miracles of the Bible never ceased.

- The power of God displayed through His miracles, signs, and wonders is available to us and happening all over the world today.

- Jesus commissioned us to continue to do what He did (participate in the miraculous) and even more (see John 14:12–14).

- We are to expect miracles as part of the Christian life.

Jesus Is in Town: *"For the kingdom of God is not a matter of talk but of power."* —1 Corinthians 4:20

- The poor and needy aren't interested in our achievements. They want only Jesus because He has everything they need.

- God's power is more than sympathy, more than an abstract idea. God's power is the person of Jesus Christ.

- We are to love Jesus, not power.

- The difference between Christianity and other religions is that they have no power and Christianity does.

- It is the power of God demonstrated in miracles, signs, and wonders that brings people into relationship with Him, not good preaching.

- We carry the power of God's kingdom as faith through love.

The Supernatural Is Normal: *"Place me like a seal over your heart, like a seal on your arm; for love is as strong as death, its jealousy unyielding as the grave. It burns like blazing fire, like a mighty flame."* —Song of Solomon 8:6

- We need to be willing to step out of the natural and start living in the supernatural of God.

- For Christians, life in the supernatural with God should be normal.

- We need to be so heavenly minded that we are actually of some earthly good.

Session Fifteen Devotions

FALLING IN LOVE

*"Many waters cannot quench love; nor will rivers overflow it; if a man were
to give all the riches of his house for love, it would be utterly despised."*
—Song of Solomon 8:7 NASB

I want to revisit the aspect of loving God yet again because it is so essential to the Christian life. We can talk about what it's like to fall in love with a person—guy meets girl and there's this attraction that no one can explain. Something explodes inside you and suddenly you're interested. No one forces you to fall in love. It's just something that happens. People get uncomfortable with the idea that we can fall in love with God in the same way we fall in love with each other because of the physical aspect of what goes along with a relationship between a man and a woman. Obviously we're not meant to have that same kind of physical aspect in our love relationship with God, but what about Song of Solomon in the Bible? It's full of all this language about physical romance between two people.

People spend a lot of time trying to allegorize Song of Solomon but it is simply what it is—a love story between a guy and a gal. So why did God put it in the Bible? Song of Solomon is in the Bible to give us a picture of the very nature of love. God is trying to give us a way to understand what a love relationship is really is all about, and He's using human terms we can relate to. God is trying to tell us that we "fall" into a love relationship with Him. We are not forced to love Him. Just like the attraction between a man and a woman who fall in love, when we fall in love with God it's something that just takes hold of us. There is no explanation. Bells go off in our head and our heart and suddenly we are in love with God and it's the most powerful love in the universe. Nothing can quench it. Nothing can take this love away from you. This is a love so pure and so strong that you'll die for it. This is the divine romance of a love relationship with God. Most discipleship training doesn't touch on this because they don't know how to approach the subject without embarrassing people. God's not trying to embarrass us with Song of Solomon. He's trying to get us to understand His love for us. God is inviting us into a divine romance.

Those who try to say that the Christian life is not romantic fail to understand what God is saying. He is taking us beyond the physical aspects of love with a vision that goes deep inside the heart, showing us what will be possible in heaven. **There is something very romantic about God that exceeds any human experience**. He is essentially a romantic. He is so in love with us that He would give us His best—Jesus Christ. That is what love looks like.

REFLECTION QUESTIONS

1. How do you feel about the idea of falling in love with God?

_____

_____

_____

_____

_____

_____

_____

_____

2. What does falling in love with God mean to you?

_____

_____

_____

_____

_____

_____

_____

_____

_____

3. What is the writer of Song of Solomon trying to say in chapter 8, verse 7?

_____

_____

_____

_____

_____

_____

_____

_____

_____

_____

MADE FOR GOD

"I have found David the son of Jesse, a man after My heart, who will do all My will."
—Acts 13:22 NASB

Over the course of my lifetime, I've listened to many descriptions and ideas about why God created us. There's lots of ways of answering the question, and most of them are very spiritual. You can say He created us for His glory, for the sake of His name, to make Himself known as holy in the world, to show His power, to change the world through us, to train us to be leaders eventually in heaven, to train us to rule the world by His side in the next dimension. But for me there is only one explanation that makes sense. I think God created us for Himself. He didn't create us just to bless us and have us do what He says. **He created us because He wants to be loved. He's romantic and He wants a partner. We are made for God**.

Most of us are more comfortable being "works based" than "heart based." We can get much more excited about "doing" for God than about being with God. We are quick to ask Him for all sorts of things for our self but slow to give Him our self. The very first commandment says we are to love the Lord our God with all our hearts. This isn't a commitment, something to be done out of obedience. This is divine romance. We were created to love Him, made for love with God.

From the start of Scripture through to the Book of Revelation, God is found seeking us, the ones He created for Himself. In the Old Testament, God's people experienced His presence in a physical building called the tabernacle. In the New Testament we dwell or tabernacle with God because He is in us by His Spirit. We don't have to go to a physical temple to experience His divine romance. We are His holy temples because His Spirit lives in us. God's divine plan in Jesus Christ has removed the veil that separated us from the One who loves us with an everlasting love. We were made for Him and now we can be fully His, receiving His divine love and giving our human love in return. This may sound like God is getting the short end of the deal, but He doesn't feel that way. He wants our hearts no matter what shape we're in. He'll take us and clean us up and get us ready to be His bride. The Bridegroom is extending His hand in love. Will you receive it?

REFLECTION QUESTIONS

1. Why do you think God created you?

----

2. How are you "made for God"?

3. What does it mean to be "works based" versus "heart based"?

MIRACLES

"Every good and perfect gift is from above, coming down from the Father of the heavenly lights, who does not change like shifting shadows."
—James 1:17

You will notice from the Scriptures that Jesus didn't promote His power. He was very understated in that way. He healed a leper and then was on to the next thing. He fed 5,000 and then kept on going to the next place. People would crowd up to Him, sick and in need of healing, and He would gently tell them, "You're healed. Go and sin no more," and just keep going. He had no public relations team, no consultants, no way to "check His ratings." He was the most powerful person in the universe and at the same time the most humble. **Jesus went about performing miracles, signs, and wonders with no fanfare, knowing that God's miracles are gifts to us.**

There is such a lack of belief in miracles today, especially in the Church. Christians who can't understand miracles or who don't receive them when they ask for them are quick to declare that they don't exist today. They go along with the incorrect teaching that miracles ended when the canon of the Bible was closed. This is a teaching that has been in the Church for centuries, but it is simply not true. We see God perform miracles all the time, and so do other people all over the world. If you read the gospels you will find that Jesus never said miracles, signs, and wonders would end. As a matter of fact, He tells us to go out and do what He did and to do even greater things than He did (see John 14:12-14). We are to expect miracles as part of the Christian life. We are to value the power of God not because it's something we can wield, but because it demonstrates His love. He is the Father of heavenly lights who does not change. Every good and perfect gift comes from Him now, today, in our time, just as it has always done throughout all time.

REFLECTION QUESTIONS

1. What value do you attach to the power of God and why?

_____

_____

_____

_____

_____

_____

_____

2. How dependent are you on miracles? Think of examples.

3. Spend time in the gospels reflecting on how Jesus displayed His power and see if the Holy Spirit reveals things that you had not seen before.

JESUS IS IN TOWN

"For the kingdom of God is not a matter of talk but of power."
—1 CORINTHIANS 4:20

What is it that makes Christianity different from all other religions? Yes, we have an ideal moral system and a superior ethical system when you compare it to other religions, and that's good, but that's not what sets us apart. The difference between Christianity and other religions is that they have no power and we do. If we go into a village that has never heard of Jesus, never heard of Christianity, and we have no power, why would they take any notice of what we have to say? They are desperate. They need the power of God to change things, not apologetics. When the eyes of someone who has been blind since birth get healed, the power of God speaks in a way that words cannot. It's terrible to come into a poor village or meet somebody suffering or hurting or enslaved by sin or addiction and have no answers. We don't have God's power. He has all the power. But we have His love, and as Paul says the only thing that counts is faith working through love. That's the power of the kingdom we carry.

Here in Mozambique, when we visit a village in the bush, people come from hundreds of miles around, walking barefoot with no food, often through horrendous conditions, not because we are conducting an amazing conference, but because they heard Jesus was in town. They don't care who the speaker is for the day. They aren't interested in our huge network of churches or the size of Iris. They don't care how well-educated we are or how many degrees we have. All they care about is Jesus. **Our job isn't to promote what we are doing. Our job is to allow God to demonstrate what He is doing.** Our job is to walk in the power of God through love. But if we don't have the raw power of God for miracles, there is nothing to tell the people about. No, power is not the main point. Jesus is the main point. Our relationship with Him is the main point, but without His power nothing works. Relationship with God takes power. Godly relationships are the effect of God's power. In fact, everything about the kingdom involves power.

I was in university with a group of scholars who had written a book, *The Power of Love and the Love of Power*. The gist of the conversation was that charismatics are power hungry and we need to realize that it's all about the power of love. My question to them was, "Does love have any teeth? Can love actually do anything?" Their answer was, "No, love has no teeth. It's just sympathy, the power of sympathy at work." It's true that if you love power you've lost the point completely, but God's power is much more than sympathy. We're not to be in love with power; we are to be in love with Jesus. Power and all that goes with it are abstract ideas, but the person of Jesus Christ is real and lovable and all-powerful. That's where we are to focus—not on power but on the person of Jesus. He is our all-powerful King, and without His power the Gospel has no teeth. For us, miracles are not optional. We need a powerful God and we have one! Hallelujah!

REFLECTION QUESTIONS

1. Why do you think the Church has such a hard time understanding the power of God for miracles today?

2. What does Rolland mean when he says that godly relationships are the effect of God's power?

3. How did the early Church grow so quickly and spread to all the known world through a handful of people with no earthly resources?

THE SUPERNATURAL IS NORMAL

"Place me like a seal over your heart, like a seal on your arm; for love is as strong as death,
its jealousy unyielding as the grave. It burns like blazing fire, like a mighty flame."
—SONG OF SOLOMON 8:6

Living in the supernatural slipstream of God should be normal for all believers. Finding God should be normal for us. Miracles should be the norm for us. **We are in the world but not of it, our heads and our hearts in heavenly places with Jesus until we are so heavenly minded that we're actually of some earthly good!** That's how we are intended to live as Christians, and yet many have a hard time understanding that kind of lifestyle. Do we encounter difficulties in the midst of this sort of supernatural lifestyle? You bet we do! People think Heidi and I are crazy to have come to Mozambique, a fierce war zone for thirty years. Heidi's mother was terribly upset with me for years for taking her daughter to Mozambique and exposing her to all the dangers here. And yes, Heidi has been hijacked, had guns pointed at her head and knives held at her throat, and been in all manner of truly dangerous and life-threatening situations. For us that is normal because we live "in" Jesus at all times. He has set Himself like a seal upon our hearts, and there He remains.

When we first made the decision to come to Mozambique, all the missionary experts and the elders and the district superintendents and the bishops and everyone tried to talk us out of it. They told us it was dangerous and foolish to go without support. They didn't understand that's exactly what we were aiming to do. We wanted to go somewhere where we had absolutely no resources, no influence, no friends, no nothing so that God would get all the glory. There is no way anyone can say that what has happened in Mozambique through Iris has anything to do with us. What is going on through Iris in Mozambique is entirely, completely, and totally supernatural. That's why we live in the supernatural. That's where God is, and that's where we have to be in order to stay in Mozambique. It's not optional for us to live any other way.

Think what it would be like if believers learned to live in the supernatural. I don't mean just on the mission field. I mean every day, wherever we are. Imagine if inner cities began to undergo the kind of godly transformation we see in Mozambique, if whole towns gave their lives to Jesus. Imagine if Wall Street began to experience God's supernatural presence, or Hollywood, or the halls of power in Washington, D.C. Imagine if people actually walked for hundreds of miles because they heard Jesus was in town and they wanted to get close to His presence, to be touched, to be healed, to be set free. I think we all want to see that but we're not willing to step out of the natural and live in the supernatural. We allow too many things to hold us back instead of simply saying "Yes" to the One who is worthy. He is waiting. How will you answer His call?

REFLECTION QUESTIONS

1. Song of Solomon says that love is jealous and as unyielding as the grave. What do you understand that to mean in terms of your love relationship with God?

2. Imagine if you will what it would look like in your current sphere of influence if you lived life in the supernatural the way that Rolland describes it. What would that look like?

3. What is holding you back from a fully supernatural lifestyle with God?

Session Sixteen

LIVING IN THE RIVER

Heidi Baker

"Fruit trees of all kinds will grow on both banks of the river. Their leaves will not wither, nor will their fruit fail. Every month they will bear, because the water from the sanctuary flows to them. Their fruit will serve for food and their leaves for healing."
—Ezekiel 47:12

It seems appropriate to conclude our study of spiritual training for the mission field by going to the "river." There is a lovely old Christian hymn titled "At the River" by Robert Lowry. In this hymn Lowry is talking about when we die and go to heaven, but you and I don't have to wait until our physical death to "go to the river." We can *die to self* and go there now and receive all that God has for us in this life to carry us through until we reach the next.

> Yes, we'll gather at the river,
> The beautiful, the beautiful river;
> Gather with the saints at the river
> That flows by the throne of God.

The river that flows from the throne is the Gospel of Christ, the living water that comes from His pierced side. This water is ever increasing, always progressing into the world and into our hearts as His grace. Wherever the Gospel is preached, souls are nourished. His body and blood are always enough to feed the hungry. When you realize that you are among the hungry, you can begin to embrace your own constant need for the water of the Gospel. The Gospel that we carry to give away to others is the same one we must partake of daily lest we wither and fade.

There was a time when Rolland and I didn't understand our own constant need for God's living water. We were busy giving it away to the point of spiritual dehydration. We were standing on the edge of the river inviting others to jump in but not jumping in ourselves.

God had to take us to a Kairos moment before we understood how to let Him nourish us constantly lest we run dry. God has a Kairos moment for you. His river is not restricted to a few special people. It's available to all who proclaim Jesus as Lord. Jesus is the one who gives us access to this river. He is the door, the gate, the way and the truth and the life.

The last two verses of Lowry's hymn talk about reaching the silver river where we encounter our Savior's smiling face as our happy hearts quiver with the melody of peace. If you are on the mission field already or contemplating going, learn the joy of "going to the river" where you will find everything you need for this life and the next.

MAIN CONCEPTS FROM SESSION SIXTEEN

"Fruit trees of all kinds will grow on both banks of the river. Their leaves will not wither, nor will their fruit fail. Every month they will bear, because the water from the sanctuary flows to them. Their fruit will serve for food and their leaves for healing."
—Ezekiel 47:12

LIVING IN THE RIVER

Heidi Baker

Rivers of Living Water: *"If you knew the gift of God and who it is that asks you for a drink, you would have asked Him and He would have given you living water."* —John 4:10

- The story of the Samaritan woman at the well from John 4 illustrates how Jesus models an encounter with the lost.

- He knows she is lost and broken in her sin, but He approaches her from a place of need so that she can relate to Him.

- He establishes a connection and then invites her to receive Him.

- In the power of the Holy Spirit she recognizes the invitation and is able to receive Christ.

Burned Out: *"I will refresh the weary and satisfy the faint."* —Jeremiah 31:25

- Life in the mission field is harsh and many people suffer "burnout."

- Burnout in the field comes when we try and minister from our own strength.

- God wants us to live from a place of His strength.

Kairos Moments: *"In a moment, in the twinkling of an eye, at the last trumpet; for the trumpet will sound, and the dead will be raised imperishable, and we will be changed."* —1 Corinthians 15:52 NASB

- A Kairos moment is that point in time when the Holy Spirit comes close in order to accomplish a special work in a person.

- God has Kairos moments for all believers.

- Allow God to give you your Kairos moments.

Session Sixteen Devotions

RIVERS OF LIVING WATER

"If you knew the gift of God and who it is that asks you for a drink, you would have asked Him and He would have given you living water."
—John 4:10

Before I share my own "trip to the river," I want to look at the story of the Samaritan woman from John 4 and her trip to the river. Here is a woman in need of the message of the Gospel who actually encountered the living Gospel. Scripture tells us that she came to the well to draw water around noon one day and encountered Jesus there. Now, notice that Jesus didn't begin by evangelizing her and pointing out her sin and her obvious need for Him. Jesus went for an encounter. He began by expressing His own need: *"Will you give Me a drink?"* He asked. Confused, she stated the obvious—that He was a Jew and therefore not supposed to be talking to her. Jesus knew before He spoke to her that this woman wasn't going to understand at first. He was modeling how we are to share His living water. You see, when God brings someone in front of us, He wants us to stop and get into that low place so that the Holy Spirit can begin to fall on the situation. That's exactly what Jesus did. He just sat there, a person in need.

The woman didn't know what to do with this Jew talking to her, so she tried to respond with a theological argument, but as the Holy Spirit fell on her, her heart began to open up. Jesus responded by saying, *"If you knew the gift of God and who it is that asks you for a drink, you would have asked Him and He would have given you living water."*

> *"Sir," the woman said, "you have nothing to draw with and the well is deep. Where can you get this living water? Are you greater than our father Jacob, who gave us the well and drank from it himself, as did also his sons and his flocks and herds?"*
>
> *Jesus answered, "Everyone who drinks this water will be thirsty again, but whoever drinks the water I give him will never thirst. Indeed, the water I give him will become in him a spring of water welling up to eternal life."*
>
> *The woman said to him, "Sir, give me this water so that I won't get thirsty and have to keep coming here to draw water"* (John 4:11–15).

At this point, the Samaritan woman and Jesus have a connection. The Holy Spirit is drawing her close, but she has this tainted personal history that she's afraid will get in the way. Jesus quickly deals with her history. "It's okay," He says. "I know all about you and it doesn't matter, because the living water I offer you—this river of God—flows in the low places." She feebly tries a little more theology, weighing the choices in her mind—should she be offended or should she open up and receive what is being offered?

And then, with the power of the Holy Spirit on the situation, she steps into her destiny. *"I know that Messiah is coming,"* she says. And Jesus replies, *"I am He."*

In front of her sits Jesus, the living water, the bread of life, the Gospel in the flesh offering Himself to her. It is her Kairos moment, and she steps into it. Leaving her water jar, she takes the living water back to her village. The Scripture says, *"Many of the Samaritans from that town believed in Him because of the woman's testimony."*

There is a Kairos moment waiting for you. Jesus wants to fill you to overflowing with His life so that you become a spring, welling up to nourish the thirsty and dying with eternal life.

> *Now on the last day, the great day of the feast, Jesus stood and cried out, saying, "If anyone is thirsty, let him come to Me and drink. He who believes in Me, as the Scripture said, 'From his innermost being will flow rivers of living water'"* (John 7:37-38 NASB).

REFLECTION QUESTIONS

1. How much are you like the woman at the well?

2. What do we mean when we talk about the river flowing in the low places?

3. Why is it important to establish a connection with someone before we offer them Jesus?

BURNED OUT

"I will refresh the weary and satisfy the faint."
—Jeremiah 31:25

Eighteen years ago Rolland and I hit a very dry place. We were exhausted and miserable and we said, "God, that's enough. We've had it." The Lord had spoken to me at the age of sixteen to be a missionary in Asia, Africa, and England, and at our driest moment I thought, "Well, we've done it. We were in Asia twelve years, in England three years, and now we've been in Africa a year and we're done. We've fulfilled our calling, and it's time for me to go work at Kmart because I'm too exhausted to stay on the mission field." I didn't want to do missions anymore. I was at the end of myself and so was Rolland. We were so very tired. All we wanted to do was rest. We were exhausted and we were tired of each other. We didn't want to be together anymore, and that's the truth. The mission field had been hard, then harder, then harder still and we were done. We actually hated mission work at that point, if you can believe that. We loved Jesus but were done with missions. In our hearts we had already quit. We were sick of being shot at, sick of machine guns, sick of being hungry, and sick of not having any money. We were sick of not having water and not having electricity. We had rats coming out our water pipes. We were hunger.

At the time we had an old, beat-up truck we nicknamed Lazarus. We would hitch an old army trailer to the back of that truck and drive across the border of South Africa to a place called Cash and Carry where we would buy dented cans of food for three cents or five cents. At the time we had 320 children to feed. We'd drive back with a trailer full of dented cans and then sit on the floor of our run down building and open up the cans and eat whatever was in them. It was almost always pineapple. At times people would give us bags of rice. We were so skinny. It was a very hard time and we lost hope. That's when Rolland decided to go to Toronto. Little did we know what God has waiting for us there.

When Rolland got to Toronto, God began working on his heart, filling it with a fresh new love. He started calling me every day. "I'm so sorry," he would say. "I love you so much and I'm so sorry." Then he came home with perfume for me. I'd never had perfume from Rolland before. He came home full of love for me like I'd never seen in him. It was a sweet time between the two of us, but then I got double pneumonia and became desperately ill. I reached a point where I couldn't breathe. The antibiotics weren't working and the doctors said I might die. I asked Rolland if I could go to Toronto for a healing conference, thinking that might help. It had helped him, so I thought it might help me too. We did not have money for a ticket, so Rolland offered to sell his most precious possession, his camera! At the last minute, God provided for one ticket on Egypt Air where smoking was still allowed. There I was, desperately ill with pneumonia, barely able to breathe, in a plane full of cigarette smoke. The plane stopped in Southern California and my parents picked me up at the airport. They took one look at me and drove me straight to the hospital where they proceeded to tell me I was in a cult. My father was crying. "We can help you," they said. "We love you. You just stay in the hospital and get well, and then it will be time to leave that crazy missionary man you married."

But I checked myself out of the second hospital and got back on the plane and flew to Toronto instead. I walked in the door reeking of cigarette smoke to talk to some people about checking into a rest home for burned out missionaries, but they were not welcoming. Because I smelled like smoke, they judged me as not fit for the missionary rest home. I was so offended. I was angry, offended, sick, and burned out. I was a mess. That's when I heard someone call out, "There's a burned out missionary here. She has double pneumonia and Jesus is healing her right now."

"Take a deep breath," they said. And I did, and I was healed! Totally healed!

REFLECTION

1. Burnout on the mission field is real and no one is immune to it. When Heidi and Rolland first went to Toronto, they had no strategy for dealing with burnout. But when they came home, everything changed. Why?

_____

_____

_____

_____

_____

2. Why did the fact that Heidi smelled like cigarette smoke make people think she was unfit for a missionary rest home? Were people correct in thinking that?

_____

_____

_____

_____

_____

3. Most of the things that were going on in Mozambique that caused Heidi and Rolland to burn out are still going on and yet they now manage to avoid the kind of total burnout that almost drove them from the mission field. Why do you think that is?

_____

_____

_____

_____

_____

KAIROS MOMENTS

"In a moment, in the twinkling of an eye, at the last trumpet; for the trumpet will sound, and the dead will be raised imperishable, and we will be changed."
—1 CORINTHIANS 15:52 NASB

In Toronto, when I realized I was totally healed from the pneumonia, I was overjoyed until they called for me to come up front. People up front were falling down, and I thought they were being pushed down. I didn't want any part of it, but I was so excited to be healed that I ran up anyway. To my horror I saw big hands come at my head and suddenly I fell down, hard. I fell out in the Spirit and everything changed. It was one of those Kairos moments when God crashes in. In that moment, in the twinkling of an eye, everything changed. I see these kinds of Kairos moments happen all the time now, to others. The power of God comes on you and fills you with His Spirit, and God takes you up into heaven and puts His destiny on your life and everything changes. I know what it is when I see it now, but back then in Toronto I didn't understand what was going on. Thankfully, God brought His Kairos moment in spite of my ignorance.

As I lay on the floor in His presence, unable to move, I saw Jesus. I saw the burning fire of love in His eyes and it forever changed me. In this intimate encounter, Jesus gave me His body and it became bread for me and for the multitudes. He gave me His blood and water from His side and it became drink for me and for all who are thirsty. He told me to feed the children, and said, "There will always be enough because I died." I heard him say it twice. Jesus Himself showed up and spoke to me, and since that day we've never said no to a single child who's hungry or dying or hurting or broken. We've said yes to every one since that day.

As I lay there caught up to heaven, the Lord spoke to me and said, "You must come deeper in the river. You have to live immersed in the river. You can't live ankle deep. You can't live waist deep. You can't live up to your neck. Come on! It's time to be immersed in My presence." God is calling each one of you to live over your heads in a place you don't understand, a place where you lose control. He wants to hear you say, "Take all of me! Take my mind, my heart, my spirit. I don't want to live dry anymore!" God doesn't call us to run dry. He wants you to run the race and win the prize, to bring the Lamb the reward of His suffering. We do that by living in the river of His presence where life never runs dry.

God doesn't intend for you to be a miserable missionary. He wants you to get to the other side. He wants your children to get to the other side. He wants you to long to live over your heads in a place of joy, beauty, and power in His presence. This is His river of life. Jump in! Put your whole self in the river! It's a glorious place to be. Go after your Kairos moment. Allow Him to change everything. He wants to put His destiny on your life, to fill you with His Spirit, to take you deeper and then deeper still. **God is looking for radical lovers who will give Him everything. Will you be one of them?**

TRAINING FOR HARVEST

REFLECTIONS

1. Revelation 22:1 says, *"Then the angel showed me the river of the water of life, as clear as crystal, flowing from the throne of God and of the Lamb."* If Jesus is the living water, then how do you get into the river of God?

_____

_____

_____

_____

_____

_____

_____

2. What does it mean to jump fully in the river with God?

_____

_____

_____

_____

_____

_____

_____

3. A Kairos moment is defined as the right or opportune moment, the supreme moment, God's appointed time. Have you experienced your Kairos moment? If not, what will it take for you to step into that moment when it comes?

_____

_____

_____

_____

_____

_____

_____

PARTS ONE, TWO, AND THREE CONCLUSION

There is a new breed of missionary being released across the earth—transparent saints with oversized hearts beating in rhythm with the heart of their Bridegroom King Jesus, carrying His glory across the earth. Fearless, laid-down lovers who know a love that has no boundaries—ones who are ready to run into the darkest places of the earth and bring in the lost, the dying, the poor, and the broken. Jesus came with ceaseless love for both the one and the masses. Now we must do the same—stop for the one, but believe for the multitudes.

The primary goal of all mission work should be to seek the face of God with all our hearts, that we might glorify Him and enjoy Him forever. As His Spirit works powerfully in us to do the works of Jesus while on earth, we aim to reveal to the world in every way possible a supernatural love that wins hearts to our Bridegroom and King. The Father has communicated Himself to us in His Son, who has become to us all we need and everything we need. As representatives of Jesus Christ we must preach the simple and pure Gospel of devotion to Him, allowing nothing to detract from the power of the cross and always bearing fruit in every good work.

We proclaim Jesus. He is our salvation, our prize, our reward, our inheritance, our destination, our motivation, our joy, wisdom, and sanctification—and absolutely everything else we need, now and forever. All His grace and power flow to us through the cross and no other way. Some may consider missionaries social workers and humanitarians, but all good works are in vain if we do not bring the lost to faith in our God and Savior Jesus Christ. We must be known by His name, first and foremost, not expecting fruitfulness to come out of anything but intimacy with Him.

Believe in the present power and desire of the Holy Spirit to guide, to teach, to inspire prophecy, to give gifts of all kinds, and to work signs, wonders, and miracles with a commitment to remain sensitive, flexible, and obedient to the day-to-day leading of the Holy Spirit, from the least of your decisions to the greatest. As God provides for us both individually and corporately, together we receive our greatest reward as members of a single people—one Body, one Bride.

Value immediate intimacy with Jesus, a life of utterly needed miracles, concentration on the humble and lowly, willingness to suffer for love's sake, and the unquenchable joy of the Lord, which is our energy, motivation, weapon, and reward. God is calling His sons and daughters to *go* into *all* the earth that His house may be full. Come and live as holy and whole-hearted lovers of God! Offer yourself up to Him, consecrating your "house" so that His name may forever be seen and heard on the earth by all peoples until He comes again.

Now my eyes will be open and my ears attentive to the prayers offered in this place. I have chosen and consecrated this temple that My Name may be there forever. My eyes and my heart will always be there (2 Chronicles 7:15-16).

PRAYER

Lord God Almighty, You have called Your servants to be instruments of Your salvation in all the world. Quicken their hearts in devotion to You. Increase their love and gratitude for all You have done and all You will do. Fill their minds and hearts with testimonies of Your mighty works. Enliven their spirits with the light and life of Your Holy Spirit until their every thought and every breath centers in You. May You find them always and everywhere in praise to Your holy name and on their knees in prayer that they may know You more and be known by You forever. May they always and everywhere be effective examples of You in word and deed, rejoicing in Your glory, protected by Your blood, sent out with the sword of the Spirit, and shod with the gospel of peace until all the world is drawn to Your marvelous light.
Hallelujah! Amen!

Part Four

MISSION BASICS:
CULTURAL ASSIMILATION, LANGUAGE LEARNING, DEALING WITH CULTURE SHOCK

by Brian and Lorena Wood

INTRODUCTION

"The Spirit of the Sovereign Lord is on me, because the Lord has anointed me to preach good news to the poor. He has sent me to bind up the brokenhearted, to proclaim freedom for the captives and release from darkness for the prisoners."
—Isaiah 61:1

"Mission Basics" is designed to help you explore concepts associated with learning a new language on the mission field, exploring a new culture, and dealing with the inevitable cultural stress that is part of the life of every missionary. People with powerful anointings from God can accomplish great things, but at the same time those who can speak the language and understand the culture they minister in will find a new level of effectiveness. When you are filled with the Holy Spirit, grounded in the Word of God, and know how to acclimate to your environment, you are better able to enjoy the journey and be of benefit to others. God wants to partner with you, and He's excited that you want to partner with Him.

In the following pages we will attempt to share from our own personal experiences in the mission field and will also present concepts gleaned from Thomas and Elizabeth Sue Brewster's classes from the Fuller Theological Seminary School of World Missions, many of which can be found in two booklets by the Brewsters titled *Bonding and the Missionary Task* and *Language Acquisition Made Practical* by Lingua House Publishers, 1976. I have not done the arduous work of citation, but instead am relying on memory and personal experience for the concepts presented herein.

We have had the privilege of training hundreds of missionary students. Typical questions from students are:

- "Do I have to be a great teacher?"

- "What if I can't learn the language?"

- "I have never been a pastor or Christian leader. Can I still be a missionary?"

- "Do I need a degree in missions?"

I always answer these types of questions with two questions of my own. First, "Do you know the basics of the faith?" And second, "Can you share the Gospel with others?" It may be hard to imagine, but a huge percentage of Christians in the world today cannot do these two things. If you can do these two things, you are well on your way to being qualified as a missionary.

When I was pastoring in the States, my brother-in-law asked me, "Would you like to come and run one of our Bible schools in Africa?" He went on to say, "The church is a mile wide but only a quarter of an inch deep. The pastors don't even understand basic doctrine." When he said this, I never thought that one of the basic doctrines h was describing was salvation!

For years as a missionary I quizzed people, "How does someone go to heaven?" More times than not I got the wrong answer. "Be a good person." "Go to church." "Stop doing evil." "Pray." "Do good things for others." I always listen for the key word, *faith*, and the most important name, "Jesus!" I have heard hundreds of people over the years explain how they think someone goes to heaven without even mentioning the name of Jesus. Now, this is understandable when talking to people apart from Christ who make no confession of being born again, but what about those within the Church?

This lack of understanding should not be surprising. Even in America four out of ten Protestants believe that salvation is earned by good deeds rather than a free gift through faith in the Lord Jesus Christ.[1] If we in the West, with so many resources, are confused, imagine areas with extremely low literacy rates and almost no Christian resources!

Let me give an illustration. We held a pastoral training seminar for all of our church leaders in the largest province of Mozambique. We invited all the district pastors from the province as well as their top leaders. These men are the leaders of the leaders. During the day we taught an inductive Bible study method to help them prepare biblical messages. At night we interviewed the district pastors. We asked them questions like, "How long have you been a pastor?" "What type of Bible training have you received?" "When did you become a Christian?" To this last question we seemed to get the same answer over and over. For example, one pastor answered, "I entered the Church in 1999." Others said similar things but of course used different dates. This led us to ask more questions, "How does someone go to heaven?" After interviewing eighteen district pastors, only two said, "Faith in Jesus." Many said, "Join the Church." One said, "Tithe and pray." Sixteen answers centered on doing good works and/or decreasing sin in one's life. After this experience, we changed the way we did ministry.

LOVE AND RESPECT THOSE YOU COME TO SERVE

Too much of what is done by foreigners in the name of missions is done from a position of superiority. "Let us show you how things should be done. We are the experts here to help the poor native." Missionaries come with translators or right out of language school as the scholars who are going to teach "the way of God more excellently." These attitudes and actions don't build bonding friendships where ministry happens naturally. Rather, they create a barrier that is hard to remove once in place. I have seen teams of well-meaning young people with very little construction experience ignore the local skilled labor to build a house or a church. With no sense of cooperation in working together with locals, the teams build their structure in record time. But have we shown love and respect for the people? It is essential to respect others in order for them to respect us.

There is such a difference when we come with humility as visitors to another country and their culture. We have been on three mission fields for almost fourteen years and I have probably said more than a thousand times to the people, "You are the experts. You know the language and the culture. I will never understand the language and culture as well as you. You not only know the national language but you are experts in the heart language of your people. Help me learn!" When I talk about preaching and teaching,

I always say, "God has already uniquely gifted you to communicate effectively to your people." Rather than being the expert, try being a humble learner.

It is better to say, "I need you," "We can't do it without you," than to come in as the authority. Even if you have a doctorate from a prestigious seminary in the US and lots of Bible knowledge, always come in as a learner, dependent upon those who know the culture and language. When you work, plan, and seek God together with the nationals, people respond to this kind of humility and respect. Everyone wants to feel valued.

RESPOND WITH ACTION

When David was sent by his father Jesse to visit his brothers on the battlefield, he had no idea he was going to fight a giant. When he arrived with the supplies for his brothers, he saw how fear of Goliath filled the camp. Trembling at his intimidating, taunting insults, the Israelites endured his threats day after day. Saul and his fellow Israelites had lost hope. Outraged at this sight, David must have said to himself, "Something has to be done about this! This is not right!"

Now we know David had faith. God created this within him through the circumstances in his life. Previously, David had fought a lion and a bear successfully. God had allowed these two fierce enemies of the sheep to attack David's flock. Both times the Lord was with David, giving him victory over an enemy that normally would have ripped a young boy apart. David's faith and relationship with God grew through these trials, step by step. He knew his Lord personally, worshiping Him countless days on the hillsides as he tended the sheep. With this intimacy, calling and depending on God in the face of fierce opponents came naturally. He learned and saw firsthand how all things were possible with his God. If we want to have an effective ministry, we too need to have faith like David, continuing to trust in God's mighty power no matter what the obstacle.

What happened to King Saul? Why didn't he take out Goliath? King Saul was the tallest man (besides Goliath) and the leader of Israel's army. In fact, he was a head taller than all the other men. He should have been used by God to defeat this giant. But Saul trembled along with everyone else. He had started out well in the beginning but did not continue in a loving relationship of faith and obedience with God. Because of his disobedience, God rejected him as Israel's leader. Instead, He chose David who was a "man after God's own heart."

Faith is important. Obedience is important. Of course these two work together. However, I would like you to see an important part of this story. This part is the missing part in the lives of so many Christians. David looked, reacted in shock, and *responded with action*. I have found that most of those with effective ministries have this perspective. For example, let's say a young couple visits Thailand for a short-term ministry trip. They see the way young girls are bought and sold in human trafficking and say to themselves, "Something has to be done about this," and they start a ministry.

When my brother-in-law told me, "We have thousands of churches, yet the pastors do not understand basic doctrine," I said to myself, "That is horrible. I need to do something about this," and I did. I looked, I was shocked by what I saw, and I responded with action. If there is something within you that cries out when you hear about missions and the needs in the world, then ask God, "What can *I* do about this?" Short-term mission trips are an excellent way to get out there and see what God sees, what's breaking His heart. So often, it is in the process of "going" that God shows you what to do. Important note—it is also in the process of doing that God often shows you what you are *not* cut out to do as well. If you have a calling to missions, then go. Don't let anything stop you. If you are mentally and physically healthy and love Jesus, then go! But before you go to some expensive Bible school or missions training school, get out there on a short-term trip to see if this is your calling.

One of the best interns we've ever had was a young man named Ben. Not only was he the best chef we had ever met, he was willing to cook for us too. But cooking wasn't the only thing Ben was good at. Having a "just put me to work" attitude, Ben sought out opportunities to minister. Invited by our many churches hungry for the Word of God, Ben began teaching throughout the district. He didn't know how to use a manual transmission, but that didn't stop Ben. I showed him, he practiced in our mango grove and then took our truck everywhere. One day he noticed a group of foreigners looking a bit lost and tired. Stopping to hear their story, he discovered this short-term missions group needed better lodging and more opportunities for ministry. They were living on dirt floors and some had fallen ill. Ben, with permission, invited them to our center where we had vacant dormitories. Half the team recuperated from malaria while the other half worked with Ben on constructing a house for a poor elderly widow. Other times Ben would visit the hospital with us, hanging mosquito nets and praying for the sick. Ben saw the needs and met them. The vast majority of long-term missionaries begin with serving on short-term missions trips. Be encouraged. Get out there. Thousands of opportunities exist. Start the car and let God drive. He will guide you!

Enjoy the journey. Continue to trust and obey as Jesus leads you into all the good works He has prepared ahead of time for you to do. His grace is sufficient and His abiding love endures forever. Remain intimately connected in Him and let His joy be your strength. Stay grounded in the Word every day. Consider ministry opportunities as a privilege—we get to partner with the Most High God in releasing life into the dying world! Hallelujah!

NOTE

1. Quote from the Barna Group: "Protection from eternal condemnation for one's sins is widely considered to be earned rather than received as a free gift from God. Half of all adults (50%) argue that anyone who 'is generally good or does enough good things for others during their life will earn a place in Heaven.' …four out of ten Protestants accept this view of salvation ensured by good deeds. Almost half of the non-evangelical born-again Christians also adopt this view, in spite of the fact that they have prayed for the forgiveness of their sins and asked Jesus Christ to be their savior—actions which they believe were the basis of their assurance of salvation. Apparently, large numbers of the non-evangelical born-again adults believe that people have a choice of means to salvation, either the grace-alone or the salvation-though-works approaches." https://www.barna.org/component/content/article/5-barna-update/45-barna-update-sp-657/82-americans-draw-theological-beliefs-from-diverse-points-of-view#.V2mYnI-cHIU.

FIVE IMPORTANT PRINCIPLES
FOR NEW MISSIONARIES

Principle #1: When arriving on a new mission field, spend the first few months socializing only with locals—not fellow ex-patriots.

Driving from the airport into Naga City, Philippines, with all our suitcases piled up and our two little girls—Marissa was three years old and her sister Danielle had just turned two—on our way through Hong Kong, we hailed a jeepney and headed to the city. No one had come to the airport to meet us and no one was waiting for us in the city. In fact, we didn't know a single person in the whole region. We had never been here before and had no clue where we were going to stay. Our plan was to stay in a hotel until we could find a small house to rent. We decided not to meet with any foreigners, determined to spend the first few months socializing only with locals.

This was not our first time on the mission field. We had done the same things on our first missionary journey to Indonesia. Again, determined not to meet with any expatriates (expats—a person temporarily or permanently living outside their own country of origin), we traveled by train from Jakarta to Bandung. Speaking to people on the train, we learned and practiced our first few sentences in Indonesian: "How are you?" "My name is Brian." "I am from the United States." "We are here to learn your language and make friends." "Can you recommend a simple hotel in Bandung for us?" "This is all I can say."

By the time we arrived, we were able to communicate our need and find a nice but inexpensive hotel. Finding people willing to talk and help us turned out to be quite easy. Being a college town, we soon noticed a small parade of college students leading us around. All of them wanted to learn English and spend time with the Americans who needed help. People love to help people in need.

Principle #2: People help people in need.

Bandung, Indonesia was our first long-term mission field. We had no living quarters arranged and no other missionaries there to meet us. This is normal in our situation, as we wanted to do church planting among an unreached people group in a country that didn't grant missionary visas. So basically this made us pioneers. The first day at the hotel we began learning and practicing how to say, "We would like to rent a room for a month. Do you know of a family we could rent a room from?" Then we went outside and began talking with everyone we could. Within a few days, we found ourselves in a wonderful home. The parents asked us to call them "Mom" and "Dad"—we were quickly "family." Sometimes "Dad" would invite us to his workplace so we could practice language learning with all his co-workers. While living there, we also picked up on many aspects of their culture, family life, and local religious practices.

Before long, it was time for us to find our own place to live. Two young men from the university came to us with a list of places to rent, ranging from $45.00 to $110.00 per month. They had already gone to the homes and arranged the prices, fearing they would go up if they talked to a foreigner. Not having a vehicle, prices were much cheaper for us. We determined to only use public transportation and therefore didn't need a place for a car or a road to get to our new house. Most of the inexpensive homes just had footpaths between crowded residences. The house we found was perfect—surrounded by the people group we wanted to minister to and at a very affordable price. This gave us another natural way to bond with our new friends. Bottom line—the locals helped us when we were in need.

Principle #3: Live as close as psychologically possible to the same standard of living as the people you want to minister to.

If you are ministering to the extreme poor, living as they do can be difficult. If your desire is to stay in your host country long term, think about what kind of house you can handle long term. You may try a very simple home to begin with and see if you can psychologically manage it before giving a long-term commitment. Safety is usually a concern and may vary depending on whether you are single or married. We chose a very simple house in Indonesia and just cleaned it up with lots of cement patching and paint. It turned out so much better for language and culture learning being in that community. Neighbors came over all day long, every day. Brian was invited to play in the local soccer team and I was invited to play with the local women's badminton team. We were both terrible at these sports, but no one cared. They loved having us in their neighborhood. Nicer neighborhoods existed in this city, but the houses were large with wide streets and walled-in yards. Neighbors didn't visit each other and no one walked the streets. They all had cars. So though we only had 500 watts in this house, no running water, and rarely any privacy, we flourished in making friends and language learning and were able to communicate freely in eight months.

Principle #4: Take only public transportation for the first year, if possible.

Cars are "isolation chambers" locking out the rest of the world, and your goal is to learn the culture and language by speaking and making friends with as many locals as possible. Public transportation is a place to practice all that you have learned, a place to interact with locals, and a way to fit in with the community. For the first eight months in Indonesia, we used only local transportation. As missionaries in the Philippines, we used only local transportation for the first fourteen months. Early on we learned all the questions and responses for using public transport. We learned how to ask for and receive directions, types of transport, correct prices, time schedules, and trip durations. Countless times we rode along with friends and neighbors to local events or shopping trips. Our goal was to learn the local language and culture and build relationships within the local community.

Principle #5: Take only what you can carry with you.

Don't ship over all your furniture and comforts from your home country. Because we had arrived with only our suitcases, we spent the first couple of weeks learning how to buy furniture with the help of our new friends. This was a bonding experience. Buying the things your host country uses for cooking, sleeping, decorating, dressing, etc., helps you begin living and looking the way they do. The sooner you can learn to appreciate and enjoy your new culture, the sooner you will feel comfortable and less homesick.

Fitting into your community will also help you with friendships. Too often missionaries create a little foreign refuge to escape back to after making quick forays into the community. While this is understandable, we need to be careful. There is a danger when we isolate ourselves in our homes. Fill your house with items that can be bought locally. As you visit homes, see what people use to decorate their homes and copy the things you like. In this way your home becomes a comfortable and familiar environment for locals to come visit.

LEANING THE LANGUAGE

LANGUAGE LEARNING THE FUN AND FAST WAY

Are you apprehensive about learning a new language? Do you want to learn a language but have discovered that it's not taught in any language school? Do long lists of grammar rules confuse you? Do you wonder if you will ever pronounce the new language correctly or remember all the new words? Do you want to be a missionary but question if you are smart enough to learn a new language? Fear not. It's not that hard to learn a new language. In fact, it can be fun. You don't have to be a linguist or a genius. You just need to learn the language well enough to be effective missionaries who can communicate to the people you want to minister to.

The following are some key principles that work for learning any language. We've used this method to learn three languages on three different mission fields and it works! If you are motivated and like talking to people, you can learn a new language. Language learning is not an academic process but a social one. The more you use words and sentences in conversations, the faster you learn them. We have found that if you use a word or sentence thirty or more times, it sticks in your brain. During our first few days we learned transportation and shopping texts. For example, "Where is the bus to Central Bandung?" "How much is the fare?" "How much does this cost?" "Could you write down the price?" (This was helpful because we hadn't learned the numbers well yet.) Though he offered, we did not take our language helper with us. We purposely didn't want to be foreigners with a guide in tow. We wanted to be people in need, humbly asking questions.

Language learning is ministry when it is done in the community. For the first couple of months, we hung out with only nationals. Later we met with a few missionaries, but not extensively. We wanted to bond with our new host culture. As mentioned earlier, I started playing soccer in Indonesia and joined the local team. They made me the goalie. Again, I wasn't very good, but the practice and camaraderie with the teammates was priceless. I took on a local name. I was Pak Subandi. Soon everyone in our area of town knew my name. Everywhere we went on public transportation, locals would shout out from the roadside when we passed by, "Pak Subandi! Pak Subandi!" At the first official soccer game where we played against another neighborhood, I was told that an extra 1,000 people came. Everyone wanted to see the American who now lived in their "barrio" play soccer! They had never had a foreigner live in their community. Many lived on the wealthier north side of Bandung with big, gated houses, but very few lived in their crowded simpler side of town.

Every day we went out into the community and practiced what we had learned that morning. The people were so gracious and friendly. Our first sentences included, "Could you help us learn your language?"

"Could we practice talking to you for a bit?" We humbly practiced and stumbled through each day. People respond to humility. They also love to feel important. Some people think language learning is something they have to get through so they can "minister." It is important to understand that when believers interact with others in the power of the Holy Spirit, they are ministering! Often the Church does not grow or participate in evangelism because Christians spend so little time with those outside the church. It is hard to love people when you don't spend time with them. It is hard to evangelize people you don't know. Jesus told us that, "No one covers up their lamp." That would be foolish. Rather, we put the lamp out in the middle of the room. I have so enjoyed spending time with people of different cultures. I like making friends. When they have needs, I like praying for them. When they are sick or their friends or family are sick, it is wonderful to be able to pray for them. It is in these encounters that God ministers to people. Locals get so excited when you speak their heart language rather than the national language. They smile and laugh; some even jump up and down with excitement! It is in those times that we find out that we are more alike than different.

KEY PRINCIPLES FOR LANGUAGE LEARNING

1. Be Willing to Look Foolish

To be a successful language learner, you must be willing to look foolish and be okay with being laughed at. You will not pronounce everything right and you'll sound like a two-year-old just learning to talk. People will think this is funny, but just join in the fun and make friends with them. They will appreciate your effort, especially if you are trying to learn their heart language.

Of course we couldn't understand most of the answers to our questions, but people were happy to point, accompany us personally, or write down numbers when trying to get directions or shop. Generally everywhere, people love to give directions and use their knowledge to help others.

2. Learn a Little, Use It a Lot

Aim to learn four sentences every day. Though four sentences don't sound like much, they multiply fast. It's important to learn these sentences perfectly, being careful to keep them at normal speed with the right pronunciation, rhythm, and melody. If a word or sentence is learned incorrectly at the beginning and you use it a lot like you're supposed to, it's very hard to correct the mistake later. When you use a word or sentence thirty times or more, it usually cements in your brain. Humbly ask your listeners to please correct you if you say it wrong. Most people are embarrassed to do this, so you really have to encourage them that this is okay and very much wanted. Two important sentences to learn right away are:

1. Did I say that correctly?

2. Please correct me if I say something wrong.

3. Find a Good Language Helper

Find someone in the community who speaks your language and the language you want to learn and "hire" them as your language helper. We find it best to never use a teacher because we don't want to be "taught" in the traditional sense. Instead we hope to prepare ideas that can be communicated effectively in the community. Find out how much a local should be paid for helping for two hours and then make sure to pay a fair amount, but not too much above the local economy. You will be spending a lot of time with your helper, so make sure you are compatible and enjoy each other's company. Hire a language helper for a week before making a long-term commitment to see if you are a good match.

4. *What Do You Do with Your Language Helper?*

a. Set a regular time for your helper to come—preferably five days a week for two hours each day.

You will soon discover that you'll think you don't "need" your language helper every day because you didn't yet master everything you've already learned. But keep him/her coming, even if you just practice together past sentences and do some drills. Staying to a regular appointed time with your language helper each day keeps you disciplined and progressing. Eventually, you'll get it! I promise. It's also not fair to your language helper to keep cancelling. You have hired that person for a job and most likely they need the money. If you must cancel, pay the person anyway.

b. Prepare what you want to learn.

Before your language helper shows up, prepare ahead of time four sentences or ideas that you want to explore and learn together. The LAMP book[1] can guide you, starting with essential basics for survival and progressing to hundreds of fascinating cultural themes. In the beginning you will just focus on what you need. As you talk to people, you will discover many things you wish you could say or come home with questions you need your language helper to answer the following day. Always have a small notebook handy to write these thoughts down as you walk around talking to people.

c. Get a "proper" translation.

Never ask for a word-for-word literal translation. For example, we would not ask Jonny, "How do you say, 'Where is the bus to Central Bandung?'" Rather, we ask him, "If I walk up to a stranger and ask him to help me find the location of the bus to Central Bandung, what would I say?" If instead you give circumstances and situations, asking for appropriate ways of making requests or responses, you will speak like a local. The better question for our language helper would therefore be, "How would you address a store keeper?" "What is the normal way to greet a stranger?"

d. Listen and mimic your helper.

The LAMP book provides several simple drills that will help you mimic pronunciation successfully. Our favorite is the "build up" drill—refer to the book for instructions on how to do this. It's quick, easy, and amazingly successful. Mimic your language helper until he/she says you are saying it right. Encourage him/her to be honest. You want to get it perfect, if possible.

e. Record your language helper saying these sentences.

At the beginning especially, you will want your helper to record the build-up drills as well as the complete sentences. If your digital recorder doesn't have a speed option, make sure your helper records both at a slower speed and normal speed. Your goal is to speak your four sentences perfectly and at normal speed. After recording, let your helper go home.

5. *Memorize Your Four Sentences*

With the help of your recorded sentences and build-up drills, try to memorize your four sentences. Repetition is the key to memorizing. Listen to a difficult word or sentence fifty times if necessary. If you have a friend or spouse learning with you, practice talking to each other. Use as many senses as possible—write it down, look at the written words, listen to the recording, and even act out what you are saying while speaking if possible. Make flash cards, tape words and sentences up around the house, create your own form of Rosetta Stone on your computer with pictures and recordings if possible.

6. *Get Out and Talk to Thirty People Each Day*

After memorizing your sentences to the best of your ability within a reasonable amount of time, get out and use these sentences with as many people as possible. You'll probably need to take along a "cheat sheet" to refer to, with your sentences written down. That's okay. Remember, you have to be okay with looking a little silly. Just try to have fun making mistakes, laughing at yourself, and making lots of new friends!

You'll get responses to your sentences that you won't understand. That's normal—don't be surprised or get too frustrated. Write these down and ask your language helper what these mean the next day. That can turn into your next language text if you desire. A good sentence to learn right away is, "That's all I can say!" after you've said your four sentences. Then say "good-bye" in the appropriate way and walk away. Obviously you won't be carrying on long conversations with people for quite a while. One of the first language learning texts outlined in the LAMP book is to get a route of listeners (preferably around thirty people) whom you can talk to each day. Going to a local market is a good place for this, but be sensitive if your listener is busy with customers. Your text at the beginning would say something like the following: "I am learning the _____ language. I will be learning a few sentences every day. Can I come by each day and practice saying these sentences to you?"

7. *Learning the Culture Happens Automatically When You Learn the Language*

You'll learn much about the culture as you learn the language. For instance, if the language has different ways of addressing an adult verses a younger person, it's obvious they give notable respect to their elders. Addressing men versus women may also be different. Think and ask questions about the cultural significance to the language variations. A culture gives words to what they value. If a certain topic has lots of words to describe it, you can be sure this is a high value in their culture. Contrarily, if you can't seem to find many descriptive words for a certain topic, emotion, etc., that culture most likely doesn't value it. As you learn the language with many varying topics of interest, you will be fascinated as you simultaneously learn the culture.

8. *Power Sentences*

Sentences that empower you to learn even more sentences are called "power sentences." These are extremely important to learn right away. Make sure you carry a small notebook with you at all times so you don't miss out on any opportunities throughout the day to keep on learning. Examples of power sentences:

- "What is this?" "What is that?"

- "How do you say _____ in _____?"

- "What is the opposite of _____?"

- "What am I doing?"

- "What is he/she/they doing?"

9. *Don't Pick Up a Grammar Book for Six Months*

As tempting as it might be to go out and buy a grammar book (if they exist for the language you are learning), don't do it! Just wait. The time will come when a grammar book will be helpful, but not in the beginning. I know this is difficult, especially because this is how languages have been taught for centuries. I remember memorizing endless lists of declensions, conjugations, and grammatical rules in high school Spanish class, yet on a shopping excursion to Tijuana, Mexico, after two years of high school Spanish, I was unable to talk to anyone. Remember, children learn to speak long before they pick up a grammar book. It is also important to note that you will probably *never* sound as fluent as a seven-year-old native speaker. Odds are very good that you will most likely make more grammatical errors than a seven-year-old native speaker who has never even glanced at a grammar book.

Lists of grammar rules and complicated conjugations are a surefire way to become totally discouraged. Instead, learn complete sentences. Have fun talking to people and making friends. Believe it or not, after about six months of full-time language learning, your brain will start noticing when something sounds right or wrong. When this natural process begins, then you can pick up a grammar book to understand the whys. If you try to learn with a grammar book first, however, you'll be too scared to just start talking; you'll be overwhelmed with too many rules.

10. *How to Speed Up Comprehension*

Your comprehension will increase more rapidly when you focus on active listening. It is amazing that people actually buy products that claim you can learn a language while you sleep, cook breakfast, or work claiming that you don't even have to pay attention, claiming that through some kind of miraculous osmosis the new language is going to enter your brain. Passively listening to audio recordings of a language you don't understand is *not* going to help you reach your fluency goals. What will work is *actively listening to sentences you can understand.*

The goal is to learn how to speak and comprehend what we read and hear. If you learn a little every day and use it a lot, you will learn how to speak in your new language. If you want to improve comprehension, then active listening can speed this up. Listening to hours of another language will not help you learn that language; however, listening to hours of a language that you can understand will help you immensely. Here is an illustration. Bob makes an audio recording of one sentence—first in his language, followed by the same sentence in the language he is learning. The sentence in English: "Birds fly high in the trees while singing a beautiful song." In Portuguese: "Os pássaros voam alto nas árvores enquanto canta uma canção bonita." If Bob knows some Portuguese and continues to listen carefully, he can comprehend the words for *birds, fly, trees, singing,* and *beautiful songs.* As he listens to this enough times, his comprehension of the language improves. I call this "active listening to what you can understand." There is no end to what you can listen to. It is important to note you are not learning how to speak through this process. You are just learning to comprehend what you hear.

Making these types of recordings can be very time consuming, but there are other options. If a visiting pastor speaks in your language and it is translated into the language you are learning, you can record this. Now you have sentences in your language and sentences in your new language. You can actively listen and understand, but be aware that the translation may not be perfect; however, for the purposes of learning, it still can be very helpful.

11. *Three Factors to Successful Language Learning*

a. Accountability

First and foremost, your chance of learning a language will increase if the organization you are a part of requires you to learn the language.

Organizations that require you to be at a certain point within a specific amount of time (or you will be sent home) have the highest rate of success in in the mission field and elsewhere. For example, within one year if you cannot tell people about yourself, share the Gospel, and carry on basic conversations in your new language, you will be sent home. These types of requirements may seem tough, but they work. However, like many things, these instructions are guidelines that can be adjusted.

If there is no formal accountability structure in place for an organization you are working for, you can create your own. Find missionaries on the field, instruct your mission board, or just choose certain friends or family from home to hold you accountable if your organization doesn't. The LAMP book gives guidelines for this if needed. Years ago I had an amazing professor who taught language learning. His name was Thomas Brewster. Something he said has been proven true over and over again, especially in the area of language learning. He said, "People do what you inspect, not what you expect." If you have a person or group to be accountable to, the more details you share with them the better. Have a regular time to meet together, whether in person or on Skype, perhaps every two weeks. Set some goals ahead of time. If possible, pick people who have been successful at language learning. Many people quit due to lack of motivation and discipline, but if you just keep learning something new each day and never stop, you will speak the language someday. If you are struggling to meet your goals, make it more fun by setting some rewards in place. Where there's a will, there's a way.

b. Sufficient Time

The second factor really goes along with the first—the amount of time the mission organization gives you to learn the language.

If you join a group that puts you to work upon arrival or if shortly after arrival they expect you to "fit in" language learning, your chances of success go way down. It may seem obvious, but language learning takes time. When we went to Indonesia and then to the Philippines, we were able to learn the languages because we had no other commitments in the beginning. Learning the language and culture and spending time with the people was our only responsibility. In the Philippines, we did not start formal evangelism and church planting for fourteen months.

Whether or not an organization has an accountability structure in place and allows sufficient time to learn indicates the value an organization places on language learning. If they say, "We want you to learn the language" but then do not give you the time or hold you accountable, it probably is not a high value or priority for that organization. If you want to learn a new language, find out how successful other missionaries within that group are. Ask them how much time you will be given to learn the language. Find out how you will be held accountable.

c. Linguistic Complexity

When we first arrived in Naga City, Philippines, our desire was to learn Bicolano. The Bicolano language was spoken by five million Filipinos, but all the missionaries learned the national language, Tagalog. We always encourage missionaries, whenever possible, to learn the heart language of the people. We went straight from the airport to a hotel in the city. From there our desire was to rent a home and learn the local language. However, in Naga City most of the people spoke Tagalog to one another. Many of the shop owners spoke a Chinese language, and many spoke English. It would have been very difficult for us to learn Bicolano in the city. After some investigation, we decided to move to a fishing village two hours from the city. Everyone in that village spoke Bicolano. Very few spoke English, which forced us to learn the local language as quickly as possible. Survival depended upon it.

If only one language is spoken in a community, your chances for success go way up. When your own language is spoken by almost everyone, your chances for success go way down. When two, three, or even four languages are spoken (not uncommon in many parts of the world), language learning becomes even more difficult. It would be very difficult for me to learn Portuguese in the US; however, if I moved to a small town in Portugal or Brazil where there were very few English speakers it would be much easier and quicker. Always try to put yourself in a place of immersion and need. If finding food to eat depends on your ability to get directions, ride public transportation, and buy the food, you'll do your best to learn these words as quickly as possible!

12. Immerse Yourself

Many years ago a course on how to swim was taught to some youth in New York City. I have a picture of a young person with his stomach down on a stool, practicing his breaststroke. The facility did not have a pool, so the students were learning in a classroom. While you can learn in a classroom, I think we can all agree it is not the best place to learn how to swim! You have to get into the water. My dad told me how Grandpa taught him how to swim. Grandpa said to my dad, "You know you can swim just by keeping your head above the water and paddling real fast like a dog." Then Grandpa threw him into the deep end of the pool. All right, that is a bit rough, but he learned to swim!

Most missionaries don't immerse themselves, but rather do things that kill the language learning process.

1. They set up a little America (or whatever their nice country of origin is) in their home and venture out only when needed.

2. They spend most all of their social time with expats.

3. They travel around in an isolation capsule called a car.

4. They see ministry as a separated special time when they leave the comforts of home or the office.

We need to understand that learning a language is primarily a social process. The more time you spend talking and listening to people, the faster you will learn the language. In order to show love to people and have an effective ministry to them, it's obvious you need to spend time with them. I am always amazed how fast single people who live with a local family learn a language. The dynamics that cause this rapid learning process are obvious. Time, interaction, and need are the key factors in facilitating rapid language learning.

Important questions to ask yourself: How can I immerse myself? If I have a family, how can I set my life so I can learn somewhat like a single person who lives with a local family? While I am learning the local language and getting to know my new hosts, do I need a car? Can I do without one, at least for a while?

13. Don't Go to Language School

Like learning how to swim without a pool, learning a language outside of the community can be a frustrating process. From our observations this is especially true for families. It is difficult to get away from the kids to attend three or four hours of language school classes. When school is over, parents need to get back to their kids, back to homeschooling, back to prepare meals, etc. Without time for interaction with the locals and using what you just learned in class, most of that information will be lost. It is only when you talk to people that a new language sticks! Remember, language learning is a social process, not an intellectual activity.

On the other hand, we have seen single people excel in language school. These are the ones who lived with a local family. They did not hang out with their expat friends and coworkers. Rather, they were immersed in the community. The things they had learned in class, they used. Putting into practice what you have learned is the key to being an effective language learner. It was not that the language school helped these individuals learn so fast. It was the amount of social interaction they had with the people. We have found that a better approach than language school is to learn a three to four complete sentences each day, learn them exceptionally well, and then go out and use it. This is the opposite of most language schools where you are taught a ton of word lists, sentences, and grammar rules, but use them very little. The key motto to remember is, "Learn a little; use it a *lot*." Don't worry if you think this is *too* little. The sentences quickly multiply and you will be conversing in no time—if you use them!

14. Learn the Heart Language

You will have a much better connection with your people if you learn their heart language. The national language in many countries is a colonial language and is only learned in school. If one doesn't go to school, he or she most likely won't speak, read, or write the national language well, and sometimes not at all. Many don't go to school for various reasons. They usually just speak their heart language to each other, at home, and among friends. Unfortunately, language schools usually don't teach heart languages. You must get out among the people to learn what is in their heart and how their language speaks their heart.

NOTE

1. Resources for Language Learning: *LAMP*, by Tom and Betty Sue Brewster. This stands for *Language Acquisition Made Practical*. It will walk you through lessons for one year of full-time language learning. *LEARN*, by Tom and Betty Sue Brewster. This sequel is a smaller booklet that can keep you going for another six months or so after you complete the *LAMP* book. We used these two books for all three languages we learned.

CULTURE SHOCK

Culture shock happens on the mission field. It comes with the territory. It is normal to feel tired and frustrated when visiting or living in a foreign country. Moving in general is stressful, and it is more stressful moving to a new culture. Everything you've always known is gone and replaced with something new, which you now need to learn and adapt to. Something previously simple, like getting ready for your evening meal, can become extremely stressful because of all the unknowns. Where is the market? How do I get there on public transportation? Why is the jeepney taking so long to come? How can we possibly all fit on that jeepney? (Hanging on the sides, some on top....) What is this strange-looking food in the market? What is that smell? What are these piles of colorful spices with no names? Should I pay the amount they are asking for or should I bargain? What is a fair price? What is this money worth, anyway? How long do I have to wait till this jeepney fills up so I can go home? I've already waited an hour and it's so hot! Finally home. Now, how do I cook this food anyway? Kids running in, "Mommy! What's for dinner?" The power goes out; you haven't unpacked your flashlights yet. The fans stop. Darkness. Mosquitos biting. Oops—forgot to buy mosquito nets and repellent. Intense heat. Squealing kids. Exhaustion. Everyone's hungry. You feel like screaming and wonder if you've just made the biggest mistake in your life coming to this foreign land.

I've just described a typical day for a new arriving missionary family. In fact, this was one of our first days in the Philippines! Culture stress is inevitable and normal on the mission field, and it's helpful to know that up front. Even the most amazing Christians on this planet (like you) will be affected. But be encouraged. Life gets easier and better as you get "enculturated." Be patient with yourself and others, as this naturally takes time.

IMPORTANT FACTS TO REMEMBER

It is normal to experience culture shock. Remember that the shock or stress of being in another country will impact everyone differently. If culture shock affects you more than others, do not think you are weaker or less spiritual. Some jump into a new culture and experience very little stress while others can feel completely overwhelmed.

Culture shock has various symptoms. These symptoms include tiredness, anxiety, disorientation, feeling inadequate, feeling like you want to go home, unhealthy fear of touch, unhealthy fear of food, unhealthy fear of being taken advantage of, weight gain, weight loss, and desire for isolation. Note: culture shock is compounded when you feel guilty about any of the above. Do not allow guilt to compound the problem.

HOW TO COMPOUND CULTURE SHOCK FOR YEARS TO COME

Without realizing it, many on the mission field compound culture shock the entire time they are in a foreign country. They remain in isolation, going outside as little as possible. They hang out with like-minded people only, usually from their own country. They don't learn the language and they stay away from local food and customs. Rather than learning new things about the culture around them, they spend hours thinking about returning home, hanging on to utopian ideas concerning their previous culture. Some even fall into the practice of unwarranted and/or exaggerated criticisms of the culture and people they have come to serve. Without a heart for the people and their country little can be accomplished.

WHAT IS THE CURE FOR CULTURE SHOCK?

There is no "cure" for culture shock or culture stress—but there are things that help. If you are tired—rest. If you are sleepy—sleep. Find ways to "escape." Get alone and talk to God. Think about how good Jesus is. Walk on the beach. Exercise. Do whatever you enjoy doing that is fun for you. Say "no" to extra obligations. Say "no" to anything extra unless it would be fun or relaxing. Politely and lovingly avoid people who drain your energy. Think of doing one thing at a time—don't worry about tomorrow. Be early—do not wait until the last minute to do things. Never allow others' lack of planning to become your emergency. Do not try to do too many tasks at once in a foreign country. You are just asking for culture stress. Remember to take it slow. Very importantly, maintain a sense of humor. Do not be too hard on yourself. Extend great grace to those around you. Even if you are fine, others may be experiencing a lot of culture stress and need your understanding and love. When people are stressed, they might get irritable and a little difficult. Bear with them in love.

LONG-TERM METHODS FOR OVERCOMING CULTURE SHOCK

Learn the language. Learn the culture and begin to understand why people do what they do. Throw away judgment and cultural comparisons—especially the idea that your culture is superior. Learn, learn, learn while trying to understand as much as possible.

Note especially how the particular culture you are in values time. Is your new culture time-oriented or event-oriented? Knowing how your new culture values time will greatly help your stress level and keep you from offending the nationals. If you're in a rural setting with the majority existing as subsistent farmers or fishermen, most likely time is not as important as events. Learn to relax when people show up "late." In their eyes, they aren't late at all. Though frustrating for the new missionary coming from a fast-paced, time-efficient country, relax and take the process in stride when it takes days of waiting in line to register your vehicle, or the checkout lady at the grocery store wraps each and every item like a present, with tape and all. Take a breath when you are getting ready to go home after visiting a far-away church and ministering for hours. Whey they ask you to please stay for lunch and you notice a live chicken in their hands, realize this is a huge sacrifice for them. Understand that it will take two hours to prepare the meal even though you are exhausted and thinking about your three-hour journey home on the dusty, pot-holed dirt road. Smile pleasantly and reply, "Sure, I'd love to," and then sit back and find ways to enjoy the process. The event of spending time together over a special chicken meal is much more valuable than getting home in a timely manner—no matter what reasons you have.

Take nothing at face value. Ask a million questions and never stop asking questions. Do not believe everything another missionary says. Many have biases from bad experiences. Talk to as many nationals as possible. Go to as many events as you can. Go to festivals and different social events. Read local literature and watch local television. Listen to local radio stations. Love people and learn to appreciate them. Find ways to have fun together. Take it slow. Relax when needed. Enjoy life in a foreign country.

CONCLUSION

FINAL ENCOURAGEMENTS

The need is great for missionaries, and there are not enough missionaries! Those who love God and have a firm understanding of the Gospel can be an amazing blessing as a missionary on a foreign field. Paul was a Hebrew scholar, but kept his message simple and focused on Jesus.

> *I did not come with eloquence or superior wisdom as I proclaimed to you the testimony about God. For I resolved to know nothing while I was with you except Jesus Christ and Him crucified. …My message and my preaching were not with wise and persuasive words, but with a demonstration of the Spirit's power, so that your faith might not rest on men's wisdom, but on God's power* (1 Corinthians 2:1-2;4-5).

You may not be the greatest preacher in the world. You may not be a dynamic leader, but you can be effective.

> *His divine power has given us everything we need for life and godliness through our knowledge of Him who called us by His own glory and goodness. …For if you possess these qualities in increasing measure, they will keep you from being ineffective and unproductive* (2 Peter 1:3,8).

Take a look and meditate on these Scriptures. Don't listen to Satan's lies—he tells everyone they are unqualified to do ministry!

Walk in the Spirit, not the flesh. Recognize your weaknesses, but don't let them stop you. Let your weaknesses lead you to a place of seeking more of God. Get into a place of desperately desiring the infilling of the Holy Spirit daily. The more you seek Him, the more God will respond. "Ask, and you shall receive." Jesus wants to fill you with His glory and power. God chooses the foolish to shame the wise and the weak to shame the strong, so that no one will boast before Him. He's just waiting for humble vessels who want to be filled and used!

Hold fast to the Word of God: *"Let your light shine before men, that they may see your good deeds and praise your Father in heaven"* (Matt. 5:16).

> *He has reconciled you by Christ's physical body through death to present you holy in His sight, without blemish and free from accusation—if you continue in your faith, established and firm,* **not moved from the hope held out in the gospel** (Colossians 1:22-23, emphasis added).

If you have a burning desire to minister, love Jesus, and know the fundamentals of the faith, there is a place for you on the mission field. You can make things happen. Find a need and figure out how to meet it. Start ministering and God will lead you. Hold fast to Him and enjoy the journey!

ABOUT HEIDI AND ROLLAND BAKER

Rolland and Heidi Baker, founders and directors of Iris Global, have served as missionaries for more than thirty five years to the world's poorest people. Heidi earned her PhD degree at King's College, University of London, where the Bakers planted a thriving church for the homeless. Rolland has his Doctor of Ministry (D. Min.) from United Theological Seminary located in Dayton, Ohio. They have lived and ministered for the last twenty-one years in Mozambique. They also travel internationally, teaching about "passion and compassion" in the ministry of the Gospel. They have written several books, including *Always Enough*, *Expecting Miracles*, *Compelled by Love*, *Birthing the Miraculous*, and *Reckless Devotion*.

FREE E-BOOKS?
YES, PLEASE!

Get **FREE** and deeply-discounted **Christian books** for your **e-reader** delivered to your inbox **every week!**

IT'S SIMPLE!

VISIT lovetoreadclub.com

SUBSCRIBE by entering your email address

RECEIVE free and discounted e-book offers and inspiring articles delivered to your inbox every week!

Unsubscribe at any time.

SUBSCRIBE NOW!

LOVE TO READ CLUB

visit **LOVETOREADCLUB.COM** ▶

HEIDI BAKER
with ROLLAND BAKER

LIVING FROM THE
PRESENCE
— CURRICULUM —

Experience the Supernatural Presence of the Holy Spirit in Every Area of Your Life!

Every follower of Jesus has received the Holy Spirit. If you have given your life to Christ, you have His very Presence living inside of you. And yet, there is still more!

What if the same Spirit Who lives inside of you could work through you with miraculous power? What if the Holy Spirit was more than a theological concept and became your day-to-day supernatural experience?

In the *Living from the Presence* curriculum, Heidi and Rolland Baker take you on a journey like never before. In eight interactive study sessions, Heidi and Rolland guide you into the manifest Presence of God where you will encounter Him face to face and be forever marked by His transforming power.

Come hungry for a God-encounter! These video sessions capture the dynamic move of the Holy Spirit in live meetings, releasing an impartation of the same Presence and power to you!

Discover How To:

- Increase your awareness of the Holy Spirit's Presence and experience His closeness in new ways
- Release the atmosphere of Heaven into your spheres of influence
- Experience new levels of God's glory and witness an increase of signs, wonders and miracles flowing in your life

Having the Holy Spirit live inside of you is an incredible honor; however, in order to walk out a lifestyle of supernatural power, you need to learn how to partner with the Spirit and see His manifest presence rest upon you every day!

Powerful Sessions Include "The Foundation of His Presence," "Living Saturated in His Presence," "Miracles in His Presence," "Making Room for His Presence," and More!

INCLUDES

8 Video Sessions • Participant's Study Guide • Leader's Guide
Living from the Presence Interactive Manual